Neocon Middle East Policy:

The "Clean Break" Plan Damage Assessment

Published by the Institute for Research: Middle Eastern
Policy, Inc. (IRmep)
PO Box 32041, Washington, DC 20007
First published in 2005 - books@IRmep.org
© Institute for Research: Middle Eastern Policy, Inc.
All Rights Reserved

Library of Congress Cataloging-in-Publication Data

Shapiro, Adam.
Neocon Middle East Policy : The "Clean break" Plan
Damage Assessment / essays by Adam Shapiro, Khaled
Dawoud, E. Faye Williams.
p. cm.
Includes bibliographical references and index.
ISBN 0-9764437-3-2 (alk. paper)
1. United States--Foreign relations--Middle East. 2. Middle
East--Foreign relations--United States. 3. Institute for
Advanced Strategic and Political Studies (Jerusalem). Study
Group on a New Israeli Strategy toward 2000. Clean break, a
new strategy for the realm. 4. Arab-Israeli conflict--1993- 5.
Conservatism--United States. 6. United States--Foreign
relations--Israel. 7. Israel--Foreign relations--United States. I.
Dawoud, Khaled. II. Williams, E. Faye. III. Title.
JZ1480.A55S52 2005
327.7305694--dc22
2005007103

Table of Contents

Foreword

Grant F. Smith is the Director of Research at IRmep and the editor of this book.

On November 26, 2003, The Institute for Research: Middle Eastern Policy held a panel discussion about the "Clean Break" plan in the Rayburn House Office Building on Capitol Hill. Streaming video of the event may be viewed online from archived videos at C-SPAN.ORG.

IRmep is a non-profit 501 (c) (3) research institute that focuses on US-Middle East foreign policy. IRmep was born of a research project in 2002 that surveyed the policy research being performed in Washington, D.C. think tanks. IRmep analysts were left with vexing, important, unanswered questions. Is a Cold War, "Clash of the Civilizations" framework for dealing with Arab states appropriate or merely simplistic? How can the US act in coalition with major European allies in the Middle East? Are American policy initiatives such as the Middle East Partnership initiative adequately funded? What are the theoretical roots of our current foreign policy? Are they correct?

To be blunt, as international researchers, we've been astounded by the paucity of relevant, accurate, and usable policy research emanating from the established think tanks that dominate every aspect of debate here in Washington, D.C. Clearly there was an opportunity.

IRmep has been specifically designed to avoid the pitfalls of the existing institutes. We won't accept research guidance or suggestions from donors. We won't accept any funding from defense contractors, because we believe, as do many in the defense industry, that it is unhealthy and even dangerous to our American democracy to have defense contractors involved in policy formulation. We most prefer to build our research budgets $39 at a time with donations from American families.

Finally, IRmep research is not produced in a self-referential "black box." All IRmep policy briefs and research notes are circulated for comment from a range of Middle East academics, business leaders, and diplomats before publication. This helps avoid "group-think" and mistakes that come from inbred ideas.

And while this approach does not generate the level of corporate funding that other institutes derive, it does create actual debate and critical thought. We've been assailed by some leading Arab thinkers for insisting in January of 2003 that democratization in the region was proceeding too slowly. We've been lambasted by Israel for insisting to policymakers in Washington that US aid and loan guarantees must be conditioned on responding to US concerns about new fences and illegal Israeli settlements.

In short, we've won few friends on either extreme of these sometimes divisive issues. However, we have continued our commitment to seeking the truth. **Because sometimes the truth is painful, and the answers are not easy.**

This book explores the consequences of a historic document. "A Clean Break: A New Strategy for Securing the Realm" is a short paper produced by the Jerusalem based Institute for Advanced Strategic and Political Studies. ("A Clean Break" is reprinted in Appendix 1.) It was created to guide then newly-elected Prime Minister Benjamin Netanyahu.

IRmep believes it is a paper worthy of analysis for two reasons:

1. Three of the "Clean Break" authors reached stellar and influential heights in the US government. Richard Perle is the former chair and a current member of the Defense Policy Board at the Pentagon. Douglas Feith is Undersecretary of Defense, and David Wurmser is Vice President Richard Cheney's Middle East advisor.

2. Although little known by the public at large, "A Clean Break" has provided a more accurate roadmap of US policy than even the so-called "Roadmap for Peace." It is both a passionate and a succinct paper, though dating back to 1996; it reveals many of the authors' core beliefs and worldviews. Although we avoid the trap that Professor Paul Michael

Kennedy of Yale University calls the "mono-causal" or all-encompassing historical explanation of US policy in the region, "A Clean Break" provides insight into the real drivers of the increasingly complex and violent US-Arab-Israeli dynamic.

The first five chapters are extracted from panel speakers' notes from a diverse group of Middle East policy observers. Adam Shapiro, an International Solidarity Movement leader, discusses the creation of facts on the ground and dangerous forces unleashed as regional actors confront a superpower hegemon. Khaled Dawoud reveals the sentiments of the Arab populations and US regional policy from the perspective of a foreign news correspondent. Lebanese political advisor Adib Farha considers erroneous assumptions of the plan, while the Syrian Embassy First Secretary Mohammad Kaddam provides a Syrian reaction to "Clean Break" ideology. Civic leader E. Faye Williams juxtaposes the American civil rights battle for justice and the current status of Palestinians confronted by hard-line American policy makers.

"Clean Break or Dirty War" is included in chapter five. This seminal IRmep policy position paper was drafted by our analysts in March of 2003 and circulated for discussion to Congress, the State Department and Executive Branch, major corporations involved in US-Middle East trade, and cultural/academic exchange groups.

Professor William James Martin then analyzes the plan's effect on derailing peace negotiations and making the case for the invasion of Iraq. The final chapter examines the "Clean Break" policy mandate on Iran and how the US can address the real issue of regional counter-proliferation and finally rid itself of damaging neoconservative influences that harm productive US policy formulation.

We hope that distilling these viewpoints into a short book puts them on the historical record. We also aspire to a broad American readership, from students of political science at American universities to casual readers browsing airport bookstores for a brief, diverse, and yet digestible analysis of American foreign policy formulation.

1
Creating New Facts on the Ground

*Adam Shapiro is an organizer with the International
Solidarity Movement (ISM). Shapiro is currently a Ph.D.
candidate in International Relations at American University in
Washington, DC. He holds an MA in Arab Studies from
Georgetown University and an MA in Politics from New York
University. The International Solidarity Movement is a
network which brings together Palestinian and international
activists and grassroots community groups in the struggle for
freedom and an end to occupation in Palestine.*

*As a Jewish-American and Palestinian-American team, Adam
Shapiro and Huwaida Arraf have led direct non-violent
protests in the region. Rachel Corrie, an ISM volunteer from
Seattle, was attempting to stop the demolition of a home in
Gaza when she was killed by an Israeli bulldozer. Shapiro has
also worked throughout the region in Yemen, Egypt, Jordan,
Cyprus, and Serbia.*

I would just like to address some of the assumptions of the
"Clean Break" and talk about some of my own experience and
what I've seen on the ground over the years, and talk about the
larger context of the "Clean Break", specifically with regard to
Israelis and Palestinians.

There are two basic assumptions of the "Clean Break" report,
which are based on complete falsehoods and almost-
fabrications in an attempt to create new realities on the
ground. And it's important to note that this "Clean Break"
report was prepared for Prime Minister Netanyahu, who—at
the helm of the Israeli government and of course responsible
for participating in the peace process during those years 1996-
1999—did more damage to the peace process, which then set
the stage, of course, for the current Prime Minister, Sharon, to
pretty much bury it.

The first assumption is that the peace process years—under the Labor leadership, the Labor Party, and notably Prime Minister Rabin and Prime Minister Barak—that these were years that undermined Zionism and undermined Israel in some way. And one of the reasons, one of the ways, that this report points to is economic policies: that Israel was suffering economically in this period, this peace process period, and that this was undermining the character of the Jewish state, the character of Zionism, in Israel.

Nothing could be more untrue.

In fact, from the years 1996-1999, Israel was reaping the benefits of a decade, basically, of extreme growth. And just like here in the United States, which was highly dependent on the high-tech industry for spurring the economic development of the United States, Israel too developed a very advanced high-tech industry, which was connected, of course, to the United States, and of course to the military-industrial complex both in the United States and in Israel, something which we, as taxpayers, continue to support, which is part of the whole...problem.

The "Clean Break" strategy, though, is also based on the foundation that it is possible to secure more land and resources in a very finite area, that being the West Bank and Gaza Strip. And in doing so, Israel will be able to reclaim and reassert its domination of the land and also of its economic status, and also its ideological underpinnings of Zionism.

What this really means on the ground is that Palestinians will lose more and more land, more and more olive trees, more and more homes, more and more water.

And to think that the "Clean Break" is somehow new in this regard is to miss the point. In fact, the "Clean Break" is an advancement of a policy that was already in place.

And it was under the very Labor governments that are criticized by this report that the expansion of settlements, the expansion of occupation, the increased construction of

1. Creating New Facts on the Ground

roadblocks, of checkpoints, occurred in the occupied territories.

One example is 1996, when I visited Jerusalem for the very first time. Just between Jerusalem and Bethlehem, there was a very beautiful hill called Jebel Abu Ghneim in Arabic and Har Homa in Hebrew. We know it now as a settlement, but in 1996 it was still mostly a hill covered with trees.

It was the desire of the Israeli government and the Israeli settlers to take this hill and establish a settlement for Israeli civilians, but also for the Israeli military as a means of constructing a military base and civilian control over the surrounding region. The surrounding region being, of course, Bethlehem, Beit Jala, and Beit Sahour, traditional Palestinian cities and towns which are primarily, or were primarily, Christian.

In 1999 when I went back after my initial visit, I saw the results of three years of these policies. Three years of policies which meant the complete denuding of this hill of all of its trees and the replacement of this natural environment with steel and concrete homes for Jewish settlers to come and live in a Jewish-only area, on land that had been owned by Palestinians.

This is the heart of the "Clean Break." This is the heart of Israel's policies of occupation and dispossession of the Palestinians, something that is certainly discussed in the "Clean Break" report, but something that, I have to stress, is not new.

This document also assumes that Israel is operating from a position of weakness and that in some way it needs to re-strengthen itself—it needs to develop a "balance of power" construction in the Middle East in order to assert and maintain its position as a regional hegemon.

However, there is a conflict. If you're a regional hegemon and you are seeking power, then ultimately what will happen is that other powers will balance against you. We are finding this in the United States in terms of our policy making. When

13

we tried to promote a policy as the global hegemon of pursuing war in Iraq, other countries which were uncomfortable bandwagoning with the United States stood to oppose this policy.

France and Germany, of course, are the most notable examples, but if we look at the UN votes, most countries of the world refused to go along with the United States in its policy efforts.

In the same way that Israel is promoting itself as a regional hegemon, as a regional superpower, it is getting to the point where other countries will seek to ally against Israel. And it should be noted that there is no alliance in the current formulation. Egypt, Jordan—if they are aligned with anyone, it is the United States. They are large recipients of American aid money and American military dollars. As such, they pose no threat whatsoever to Israel.

Even Syria, which is seen as Israel's prime enemy in the region, responded to the recent bombing of an empty camp outside of Damascus with, as one parliamentarian said in the Syrian parliament, "we must assess whether there are benefits to using military force, because we've learned from the past that sometimes when we used military force, there are absolutely no benefits."

So there is quite a real understanding in Syria today that there is no military response to dealing with Israel. And I think ultimately that we will see, if not in the near future, then soon thereafter, an attempt by the Syrian government to reengage in peace negotiations with Israel.

I would now like to touch on getting into this notion of a "Clean Break" and how it is actually happening today.

This policy recommended by Mr. Perle and Mr. Wurmser and Mr. Feith did not conceive of something that was actually conceived by the Labor government, and this is why I want to point it out. "A Clean Break" is not just something for the

14

1. Creating New Facts on the Ground

Likud party, or for the Neocons, it is also for those in the so-called "peace camp."

Today there is a wall being constructed in the West Bank, and there is also a wall being constructed in Gaza. This wall is dispossessing Palestinians of their land, of their homes, of their means of survival. It is also dispossessing them of their water resources, the very material that they need to survive on this land. An estimated 200,000 Palestinians will be completely, directly affected by the wall, and who knows how many hundreds of thousands of others will be affected, given that the water resources being confiscated by the Israeli government today provide 50 percent of the water for the entire West Bank. At least 10 percent of the land of the West Bank is being annexed to Israel. And already, we have had reports from farmers who have produced documents issued by the Israeli military, telling them that if they wish to get to the land on the other side of the wall, they need to apply for a permit to enter Israel. So already, in just naming the area confiscated by this wall, it is no longer considered Palestinian land by the Israeli government, but rather, Israel.

Basically, this wall will create an untenable situation in the West Bank. 200,000 Palestinians who currently live off of the land, who are farmers, who do not need to rely on working in Israel or jobs in the Palestinian economy, who are basically self-sufficient, will now be thrust into the labor market, a labor market which is already seeing 70 percent unemployment.

Separation is the new euphemism used in Israel today; there are lots of calls for separation, and we can replace "A Clean Break" with the word "separation" today; the two are the same sort of policy. Separation is a policy that was first announced by Prime Minister Barak. This idea that you can separate Israelis and Palestinians completely, so as to secure Israel, is such that this has meant the construction of this wall.

However, we have seen on the ground, as walls, as cities are being surrounded by the wall, as villages are being completely cut off from any access to the outside world, and as Palestinians are essentially being made prisoners in their own homes, that separation, or "A Clean Break," is basically a word for ghettoization or bantustanization. And this is true for both Christians and Muslims among the Palestinian population.

The "Clean Break," then, is actually an attempt to tame America's foreign policy to suit Israel's interests. And we should acknowledge that this report—while to the letter it may be, some of the assumptions it makes, some of the conclusions it reaches, are outdated or outmoded—the spirit of the document, the spirit of the policy, is still very much alive and in effect.

Already, we have seen the lack of influence of the United States government, of even President Bush, in the wake of September 11 and his renewed popularity. He was at the height of his support here in the United States, and perhaps even internationally, when he called upon Prime Minister Sharon to evacuate from operation "Defensive Shield" and the re-taking over military of the entire West Bank. When President Bush issued the orders to leave based on the strategic consideration by the United States, Mr. Sharon ignored the order, and waited, and demurred, and waited, until weeks later, until hundreds more people were killed, towns, villages completely devastated, and another cycle of violence unleashed upon the entire region.

Perhaps this is because Mr. Sharon knows that people like the authors of this report, Mr. Perle, Mr. Wurmser, Mr. Feith, are in positions of power, are in positions of influence, such that the words of Mr. Bush, the words of Secretary of State Powell, and even today, with regards to the wall, the words of Condoleezza Rice, are merely friendly suggestions or just sort of "remarks" and not real strategic imperatives as they are formulated by the Bush administration.

I'd like to conclude by making a few alternatives, posing a few alternatives for policy, and also pointing out one thing that was somewhat alluded to by my colleagues, which is public opinion in Israel.

1. Creating New Facts on the Ground

Public opinion in Israel has consistently shown that people are willing to give up land for peace. That people are willing to end the occupation in exchange for peace with the Palestinians. This is a result of, probably, most people being tired, most people being ready to raise their children, not with the notion that they have to go serve in their army and fight in a war at some point, but rather looking forward to a time in which peoples of the region can actually live and coexist together. Despite 70 percent of Israelis polled consistently for the past decade saying that they are willing to give up occupation, to give up settlements for peace, United States policies and Israel's policies have been to promote the 30 percent that do not support giving up occupation. This 30 percent is materialized and realized with over 400,000 settlers in the occupied territories today, a number that continues to expand despite the ongoing violence, despite the casualties and the injuries and the reports of terror against Israelis. These numbers continue to increase; the numbers of settlements continue to increase.

Our policies of this country are not finding affinity with the peacemakers or the people who are trying very hard to promote peace in their lives, particularly in Israel, but rather are finding affinity with those who will continue to agitate, continue to aggravate, and continue to abuse the rights of Palestinians.

So, what can we do?

One thing, as Americans, we can do is stand against occupation and support the Israeli majority.

Again, most Israelis are opposed to the occupation, at least as they are polled. We must find a way to support them and to support ending the occupation that will allow Israelis and Palestinians to coexist in peace. Doing so will join the United States in an international consensus against occupation. It is not that there is disagreement in the international community about occupation. In fact it is only the United States, Israel, and perhaps Micronesia that continue to support UN resolutions against ending occupation. What we need to do, then, is stop funding it. US \$6 billion (per year) of American taxpayer money continues to go towards funding Israel's occupation of the Palestinians.

I can think of many better things that this money can be used for, including underfunded projects in our country: health care, Medicare, and No Child Left Behind.

Another thing we can do through this policy is make Israel safer and less exposed to violence. As even a Hamas leader said in 1999, when it looked like peace might be around the corner, his prediction for the future, if there was a peace agreement made and a Palestinian state established, was that even Hamas would be forced to work within the Palestinian community toward building and establishing a state and building and establishing a society as independent and free and viable in the world. This is something that most Palestinians would be engaged in, and something that even Hamas recognized would be the strategic imperative of the Palestinian people.

Finally, our policies must be designed to support the peacemakers on the ground. I and my work with the International Solidarity Movement have proved nonviolent resistance is an effective means of working against oppression, of working against occupation. We, however, the nonviolent peacemakers, are not supported by the United States government. The case of Rachel Corrie, of course, is the most egregious, and the most documented case where the United States government has completely failed its citizens and sent the completely wrong message to those who would choose nonviolence over violence. The American government's failure—including this Congress's failure to call for an independent investigation into the death of Rachel Corrie and expose those responsible for her killing—has shown weakness, cowardice, and basic blindness to what is an ongoing policy to liquidate not just the terrorists who are running around, supposedly, but more importantly, people who are choosing nonviolence, people who are not getting involved, as measured by the thousands now of Palestinian civilians who have been killed sometimes just walking outside their homes, breaking curfew to get to the hospital.

The only responsible policy at this point for the United States and the American people is to call out loud and clear to the American government, to our policy makers, to say, "Bring down the wall, end the occupation, and support the peacemakers."

2
Palestine Postponed

Khaled Dawoud is Washington bureau chief for Al-Ahram, *a newspaper covering Washington, DC politics and stories related to the Middle East. Since 1988, Dawoud has reported for such international news agencies as the Associated Press, Reuters, and the German News Agency (DPA), and has worked as a regional editor at* Al-Ahram Weekly. *In the latter capacity, Dawoud visited Ramallah and covered the April-March 2002 incursion by Israeli forces into Palestinian territory.*

Dawoud is an alumnus of the Adham Center. Despite his focus on TV journalism at the Adham Center, Dawoud's career to date has been largely in print journalism. Beyond his role as an Arab journalist in Washington, DC, he also works as an analyst and liaison to US media, think tanks, and intellectuals in order to explain the Arab point of view on critical issues such as Palestine, Iraq, and the impact of American regional policy.

I am speaking in my capacity as a reporter who has covered the region for about 15 years. I hope you will take my remarks in the framework of observations by a reporter who has worked mainly for Western news agencies, besides being an Arab myself who supports the Palestinian cause.

My reading of the "Clean Break" paper that we are discussing today is that it is mainly a prescription for war and long-term instability in the Middle East region. Its writers, when I read it as an Arab, give me the impression they are asserting a supremacist view based on their ideological stand and strong support for Israel. The issue is not only they support Israel, they believe in it. That vision comes at the expense, of course, of our vision, our stance as Arabs that live in the region.

Many of those who wrote this paper are in the present US administration. I have to admit that definitely September 11 was a turning point in this administration. And it did allow those whom we call the neocons who existed in the administration to push forward their agenda. But their agenda had already been there. The agenda is of those who believe it is not necessary in the present circumstances to solve the Israeli-Palestinian conflict; that, with the passage of time, the circumstances will always be more favorable to Israel's conditions.

And that is where, in my opinion, the real problem lies.

In my interviews with US officials, they do not want to take seriously our appeals as Arabs on the necessity of solving the Israeli-Palestinian problem. They think there are other matters to which we need to give priority. We talk to them about the Palestinian conflict, because they do not think it is urgent. They say, "Okay, but you better concern yourself with democracy first." I think, worldwide, there is a growing support of the Palestinian people and their cause. But they don't want to understand the genuine feelings of the Palestinian people. They (US officials) prefer working on "the priorities," priorities that those who wrote this paper have clearly reflected.

What we are seeing written in this paper is a reflection of what really happened after September 11, which started with the US initiating the war with Iraq. My reading of the way the US is conducting its policy is, the long-term objective is of restructuring the region. This long-term vision, as expressed in the "Clean Break" paper, is of doing away with certain regimes. Within this process of restructuring the region, there simply won't be a settlement of the Israeli-Palestinian conflict. They don't want a settlement now. They want to expand the building of settlements in the Palestinian territories.

They think we can shelve, a little bit, the Palestinian issue. After Iraq we will work on Syria. And then Syria becomes a regional conflict issue. And after Syria comes Iran. And the plan goes on and on and on, because in the long term, we will end up without a settlement to the Palestinian cause, because they (the neocons) feel this will serve their cause.

There is sincerely and deeply a strong sense of dissatisfaction among the Arab people. In the Arab world where I come from, I am amazed sometimes at the amount of frustration those people have—as I cover the military trials, or other trials, and there are deep convictions that what they are doing is in service to a big cause. I just hope that US officials, and the Israeli population as well, do put into consideration the recent opinion polls that we see, such as the Pew research poll. When you go to Egypt, which is a very strong ally of the US for the past 25 years, when you go to Jordan, when you go to Saudi Arabia, you find that people are favorable to the US.

I hope that US officials do not take lightly these types of points of view. Because if the US begins to implement the points in this paper, this "Clean Break" policy, we are facing a very strong opposing public opinion to US policy. The "Clean Break" policy initiatives are not going to be successful and are likely to produce more conflict in the short term, to say nothing of the long term.

I was in the occupied Palestinian territory by coincidence when Mr. Sharon reoccupied the entire West Bank in what was called "Operation Defensive Shield." As an Egyptian who has been observing how the Palestinians live and how the Palestinians suffer, one cannot but have a sense of understanding of what they consider to be a very just struggle. Because, in their opinion, they are facing the threat to their existence; they are facing daily the possibility of being removed from this land.

But what surprised me most about the way Israel conducted this operation was that it was not aimed at running after a certain number of terrorists or arresting a certain number of people. It was like collective punishment for the entire Palestinian population. When one sees Israeli tanks destroying the electricity lines, the water tanks, the destroyed cars standing parked in the streets, for no particular reason. And then think of yourself as a Palestinian; think of standing there and seeing the Israelis doing this to your city.

2. Palestine Postponed

I was once standing in front of Ramallah Hospital. And in front of the Ramallah hospital comes this poor woman, about fifty-five years old, and she is suddenly being shot down by a sniper. Probably because she broke the curfew; I don't know exactly what the circumstances were. Suddenly, this woman, who could be my grandmother or aunt, because we speak the same language, we look alike, is dead. Think of what her children are going to think. Even as an Egyptian, I had to queue every day in order to be able to cross from Ramallah to Jersusalem. I had to strip my clothes every day, and a trip which should be ten minutes takes two or three hours. I had to obey the instructions of the soldiers standing by the roadblock.

I have to think of the feelings of those Palestinians and how the current policy of "peace through strength" that people like Mr. Feith and Perle believe is going to work. I remember that Secretary of State Powell, in an interview, commented on Israeli targeted killings, how they understand about killing a "ticking bomb," because he is going to make an attack. But what about innocent bystanders killed in the process? The end result, even according to Mr. Powell, is that it is creating even more people who hate Israel. It is creating more people willing to sacrifice their lives for what they see as a just cause.

I want to conclude with the growing opinion within Israel itself that their treatment of Palestinians is inhuman and that it is not serving their long-term interests.

I have an article from Avraham Burg—he is an Israeli parliamentarian, and belongs to the Labor Party, of course, the peace camp.

But again, he makes the point that simplifies how the mindset of the Arab or Palestinian works. "We could kill a thousand ringleaders and engineers a day and nothing will be solved, because the leaders come up from below—from the wells of hatred and anger, from the 'infrastructures' of injustice and moral corruption."

So that's the problem.

What the US has done, unfortunately, by invading Iraq and implementing the policies of this paper, "A Clean Break," is they are increasing the hatred against the United States and not opening possibilities for positive change in that region.

We need peace in the region. We need a just peace. And this peace is possible. This peace is not impossible. The two-state solution can be implemented. There are people inside Israel who support it; but inside the Arab world, those people who support peace with Israel need some encouragement. People in the Arab world need some credibility with our people. When I tell them "Let's have peace with Israel," they ask me, "What is Israel doing?" They see me speaking English, and in good relations with the United States, but I get them nothing from the United States, I am not selling them anything. I am just telling them words.

The situation is getting worse on the ground. We need to encourage peace camps in both Israel and the Arab countries and to seriously work toward implementing peace now. Because **that** is the real ticking time bomb, and not the recommendations made in the "Clean Break" paper.

3
A View from Lebanon: Conflicts of Interest and Loyalty

Adib Farha is the adviser of the Lebanese Minister of Finance, a professor at the Lebanese American University in Beirut, Lebanon, and a member of Lebanon's National Audio-Visual Media Council. For many years he served as a member of the advisory team of Lebanese Prime Minister Rafic Hariri.

He lectures regularly at major academic institutions and is also a commentator and economic and political analyst, with frequent contributions to Lebanon's only English-language newspaper, The Daily Star, *and various Arabic-language newspapers, e.g.* Nahar, Safir, Mustaqbal. *His articles are frequently carried by global news agencies. He has also contributed to the* International Herald Tribune.

Mr. Farha is a frequent guest on Lebanese, Arab, and international radio and TV channels, including CNN International and BBC.

The document we are here to discuss, "A Clean Break: A New Strategy for the Realm," was originally written by the "Study Group on a New Israeli Strategy Toward 2000" of the Institute for Advanced Strategic and Political Studies. The group leader was Mr. Richard Perle of the American Enterprise Institute and seven other individuals known for their strong sympathy and blind support for the State of Israel.

We wouldn't be here today studying this document had it not been for the fact that three members of the group have since become key players in the current American administration. Mr. Perle is the former chair and a current member of the Defense Policy Board of the Pentagon; Mr. Douglas Feith, another member of the Group, is the Undersecretary of Defense; and Mr. David Wurmser, yet another member of the same group, is an adviser to Vice President Richard Cheney.

In other words, leaders of the same group that set out to draw a strategy in Israel's interest are now key players in drawing the American strategy. The underlying, albeit wrong, assumption is that American interests and those of Israel are one and the same. Accordingly, Israel's strategic interests are shaping US foreign policy in the Middle East, the world's most volatile area. The conflict of interest and of loyalty is incontestable.

I will attempt to demonstrate that: a) The strategy drawn in the said document is ineffective; b) that the document has become obsolete, since many of its underlying assumptions are no longer true; and c) that US interests are not one and the same with Israel's interests, despite the so-called "special relation" that exists between the two nations. I shall address key points in the document in the same order in which they were written.

For starters, the document states that "Israel has an opportunity to make a clean break and forge a peace process and strategy" that replaces comprehensive peace with a traditional concept of strategy based on "balance of power." It advocates the "right of hot pursuit for self defense into all Palestinian areas and nurturing alternatives to Arafat's exclusive grip on Palestinian society."

This is a clean break indeed from UN Security Council Resolution 242, from the principles of the Madrid Conference, and from subsequent initiatives that were all based on the principle of "land for peace." Most recently, it is contrary to the principal foundation of the Road Map, which was approved by the UN Security Council a week ago.

The majority of Israelis realize that "peace for peace" is a non-starter and will never deliver the peace that both the Palestinians and the Israeli people want so badly. The only result of Israel's "hot pursuits" has been fuelling the Palestinian uprising and bringing more bloodshed amongst innocent civilians on both sides.

Although Prime Minister Sharon refuses to admit it, recent polls indicate that the majority of Israelis believe that Israel would have to give up occupied Palestinian land to attain peace and security. The only disagreement among Israelis on this issue is how much land to give—and definitely not on the issue of whether or not to give occupied land back.

Indeed, all Palestinians insist that "land for peace" is the only foundation of any peace agreement. The only conclusion one can draw from Sharon's insistence on pursuing a "strategy based on balance of power," as the document recommends, is that he is not sincere in the pursuit of peace. Brute force has only brought disaster to the Palestinian people and to their economy, and the same for Israelis and their economy.

The document refers to "a continuity of values with Western and Jewish tradition." However, this continuity of values is not exclusive to Jewish traditions, which I revere out of respect for all religions. It exists equally between the combined Christian-Muslim ethos of Arabs (Christians as well as Muslims) and Western values. It is a farce to speak of continuity of values in this respect and thus imply that such continuity is exclusive to the Jewish traditions, as if Christian and Muslim traditions were different.

Followers of the three monotheistic faiths share the same basic values. However, Muslim-haters (and I am an Arab Christian, by the way) try to paint an evil picture of Islam through selective retrieval.

Prime Minister Sharon cleverly developed the strategy of Mr. Perle and his co-authors after 9/11 to characterize Israel's state-sponsored terrorism against innocent Palestinians as one and the same as President Bush's campaign against Al Qaida. But Al Qaida has no legitimate claim against the United States, the US has every right to fight its hateful venom and its horrific terror. Palestinians, on the other hand, are a people that have been uprooted from their land, who have their God-given right to fight occupation—provided, however, that they do not target innocent civilians, an act that is condemned by the same God of Christians, Jews, and Muslims.

Under the subheading "Securing the Northern Border," the document speaks of striking "Syria's drug money and counterfeiting infrastructures in Lebanon." I admit that there had been drug money and counterfeiting during the Lebanese civil war and in the early years thereafter. Some of the drug trafficking, by the way, was done through Israel. At any rate, the international community, through its specialized agencies such as GAFFI and others, has attested that Lebanon is free of both. So that statement is obsolete.

It goes on to recommend "striking Syrian military targets in Lebanon and should that prove insufficient, striking at selected targets in Syria proper." On this point, the writers of the report had the satisfaction of witnessing their client adopt their recommendation. The unprovoked attack on a barren old training camp in a suburb of Damascus almost two months ago was the latest of such brazen incursions. And how did the US administration react to that invasion of both Lebanese and Syrian airspace and the killing of an innocent guard? Nothing more than lip service calling for "self-restraint," effectively accepting the trespassing into another country. Heaven forbid that the US administration would issue a condemnation. Israel's former advisers, who now advise the American administration, would definitely veto any such thing!

The paper also alludes to capitalizing on Syria's poor relations with neighboring Turkey and Jordan. After some tension with Syria in the last decade, mainly over the presence of Kurdish opposition leader Abdullah Ocalan in Syria, Syria and Turkey have long since made up and enjoy an amicable relationship. More of the same is true between Jordan and Syria. The two young rulers of these two countries have forged an excellent relation based upon mutual respect and non-interference in each other's internal affairs. So, obsolete again!

Then, in an effort to escalate anti-Syrian sentiments among the Lebanese who have reservations against current Lebanese-Syrian relations and to entice Lebanese dissidents to bank on Israeli support, the paper refers to "Syrian tutelage" in

3. A View from Lebanon

Lebanon and to the so-called "Syrian-controlled Bekaa Valley."

The whole world needs to understand that any outstanding issues between Syria and Lebanon can and should only be resolved by the two countries' leaderships. Syria is in Lebanon because we, the Lebanese, through our elected government, asked it to come to our rescue and to help us reinstate stability, and its presence in Lebanon has cost it a great deal in blood and in money. It remains in Lebanon because the majority of the Lebanese have decided that its presence continues to be a security need, which we consider necessary, legitimate, and temporary.

The document makes the added false accusation that the Bekaa Valley in Lebanon has become to terror what the Silicon Valley has become to computers." Hogwash! Ask any foreign news reporter who has toured the Bekaa Valley on his/her own, and they would attest that they have seen no such thing. Let me refer you here to the many articles on this matter by Robert Fisk of the British newspaper *The Independent*. Mr. Fisk has toured the Valley unescorted many times. He has repeatedly denied the existence of any so-called terrorist camps. And if so-called terror bases were truly there, does anyone have any doubt that Israel would have struck at them? Regrettably, the American mindset accepts Israeli propaganda as Bible truth.

Under the subtitle "Moving to a Traditional Balance of Power Strategy," which is a nice euphemism for "Moving to a Brute Force Strategy," the document suggests that "Israel can shape its strategic environment, in cooperation with Turkey and Jordan, by weakening, containing, and even rolling back Syria. This effort can focus on removing Saddam Hussein from power in Iraq—an important Israeli strategic objective in its own right—as a means of foiling Syria's regional ambitions."

True to their recommendations, the writers of the report, who have since ascended to significant power in the administration, and like-minded people in the administration helped formulate the policy to hit Saddam at the first opportunity. According to Bob Woodward of the *Washington Post*, in response to President Bush's question during his first meeting with his senior staff on that infamous day of 9/11 of what to do next, the answer quickly came: "Let's hit Baghdad."

When an objective observer studies the document, one can reach the conclusion—as many around the world have surmised—that the decision to strike Iraq had already been taken and that the justification for such a strike came later and in a very confused manner. There was first the suggestion that the tyrant of Baghdad had colluded with Bin Laden. That has not been proven yet, as Dr. Condoleezza Rice assured us a couple of weeks ago. Then it was that he had weapons of mass destruction. Yet finding those remains elusive, and the WMDs remain a mirage. Then the goal shifted to bringing democracy to Iraq, and thereafter to the Middle East. Yet the only thing that has been brought to Iraq nearly eight months after its so-called liberation is anarchy, misery, and turning that country into a magnet for terrorism. It is noteworthy that President Bush, at the War Summit in the Azores, announced that even if Saddam were to abdicate, the US would still hit Iraq.

That Saddam was an evil man is incontestable. He should definitely have been toppled a long time ago. But it appears to many observers, particularly after reading the document we are here to discuss, that the real reason the US and its allies have gone to the trouble and expense—paid for in the blood of their brave soldiers as well as untold billions of dollars—was to achieve an Israeli strategic target that the writers of this report had set. This perception is contrary to America's interests and hardly wins it the hearts and minds of Arabs or Muslims.

Then, under the same subheading, the report goes back to the theme of destabilizing Syria's role in Lebanon. I quote, "Diverting Syria's attention by using Lebanese opposition elements to destabilize Syrian control of Lebanon," end of quote. This is the epitome of wishful thinking, lack of historical perspective, and poor foresight. Attempts to destabilize Lebanon are not in the interest of Lebanese and Arab-American relations, either, and are detrimental to US interests in the region. However, it would destroy the model of peaceful coexistence between Christians and Muslims that has survived centuries of Lebanese history and give credence to Israeli propaganda of the impossibility of coexisting with Muslims.

During the Lebanese civil war, some injudicious Lebanese Christians believed the Israeli line that since Israel is a Jewish minority in a sea of Arab Muslims, it would back the Lebanese Christians, who are themselves a minority in Lebanon. The subsequent cooperation between those imprudent Lebanese and Israel extended the Lebanese civil war. However, the same misguided Lebanese who cooperated with Israel have since discovered their grave mistake. When the Israeli-backed President of Lebanon in 1982 dared to disobey then-Israeli Prime Minister Begin's orders to sign a peace treaty with Israel outside a comprehensive settlement of the regional conflict, a building in which the President-elect was meeting with some of his supporters was bombed and Israel's disobedient ally vanished. It is useless for Israel to attempt to dupe the Lebanese one more time. They have learned their lesson and do not trust it any more. They have since discovered that Israel had in fact been manipulating them and that there cannot be normal relations between Lebanon and Israel before a permanent, just, and comprehensive settlement to the regional conflict is reached.

Therefore, when Israel invaded Lebanon in 1996 in the so-called "Grapes of Wrath" operation, Lebanese were totally united against Israel. Christian churches, schools, and orphanages sheltered their Muslim compatriots from south Lebanon who had fled north from the Israeli invasion.

Under the subheading "Changing the Nature of Relations with the Palestinians," the document suggests that "Israel may also want to better integrate its own Arabs." Ironically, the recent buzzword within the Israeli establishment is the transfer of Israeli Arabs outside Israel. This advice, perhaps the only sound one in the entire report, has been rejected by Israel.

The final section addresses "Forging A New US-Israeli Relationship." It suggests that Israel should "announce that [it] is now mature enough to cut itself free immediately from at least US economic aid and loan guarantees, which prevent economic reform" because "self-reliance will grant Israel greater freedom of action and remove a significant lever of pressure used against it in the past."

First of all, there has hardly been any significant American pressure on Israel in nearly fifty years. The only exception was when President George Bush, Sr. temporarily froze US $10 billion in government guarantees to Israel in 1992. But soon after he took that brave decision, the man who had led America to victory in the first Gulf War and restored freedom and sovereignty to friendly Kuwait lost his reelection bid. I am well aware that the economy also had a major role in that loss, but I seriously doubt that his son or any other US President would repeat the same mistake again in the foreseeable future.

Second, the notion of Israeli economic self-reliance might have made some sense in 1996, when the report was delivered. The Israeli economy had been booming for the previous several years, and Israel's GDP had witnessed impressive growth. However, since then, and partly because of the second intifada that Sharon's premeditated provocation sparked, the Israeli economy has been growing at a much slower rate.

Here, again, this recommendation has been proven both obsolete and false to start with.

Brute force from one side will only draw the same from the other side. In the meanwhile, the blood of innocent Arab and Israeli men, women, and children continues to be shed unnecessarily; both the Arab economy and Israel's continue to suffer; budget expenditures that should be earmarked for

3.   A View from Lebanon

social and economic development are being diverted to defense spending; terrorism is rapidly on the rise; and world peace remains elusive.

Besides domestic problems related to poverty, poor economic performance, and high illiteracy, the Arab-Israeli conflict is the core issue in the region. Only by resolving this chronic issue can there be peace in the region, and indeed in the world, and only then can we all start winning the war against extremism. Unfortunately, America is perceived to be blindly supportive of Israel, whose daily trampling on the dignity of Arabs and denying their human rights breeds humiliation and frustration among its victims.

The US is perceived to use double standards in its approach to the Arab-Israeli crisis. This perception is not limited to the few people who are ideologically opposed to the US. It is equally prevalent among those who have great respect for American principles of freedom, justice, and respect for human rights and those who strive to emulate the so-called "American way of life."

In fact, admirers of American values are perhaps the most vociferous critics of American policy in the Middle East. The root cause of their bitterness lies in what they see as a double standard wherein the US practices its noble values domestically but ignores them in its foreign policy.

There is but one solution that can serve America's objective of quelling the escalating breeding ground for extremism in the Middle East and the attainment of world peace, including our long-troubled region at the same time. That solution has to be based on the principles of the Madrid Conference, namely land for peace, a comprehensive solution to the entire Arab-Israeli conflict, and a fair and just solution for the Palestinian refugee problem. This has been developed further at the Arab Summit Meeting in Beirut a couple of years ago and came to be known as "The Beirut Declaration." It was reiterated with some modifications, once again, exactly one week ago when the United Nations adopted the Road Map, which is more or less the same in principle.

As such, the only American strategy that could lead to peace in the Middle East, eradicate terrorism, preserve America's interests in the region, and win the hearts and minds of the peoples of that troubled region is an even-handed Middle East policy that leads to a just, permanent and comprehensive peace.

4
A Syrian Perspective: Peace is Dangerous for Israel

Muhammad Kaddam is First Secretary of the Syrian Embassy in Washington, D.C.

We see the "Clean Break" as a nice piece of fiction literature, rich with ideology, that runs contrary to the interests of the people of the region and contrary to the traditional policies of the US in the Middle East. It is based on the concept that peace is dangerous for Israel and trying to promote this idea that peace can be only achieved through dominance, hegemony and power. That ensues the perpetuation of occupation, the perpetuation of injustice to the Palestinians and to the Arabs.

And I don't think that in the end this will serve the interests of anybody, either in the US or in the region.

We believe that the document is self-defeating. This is good news, maybe. The bad news is that some of the "Clean Breakers" are well-connected and powerful now in Washington. It was written in 1996 to foil the Middle East peace process, to foil the international and American-led effort which was based on the concept of "land for peace" and UN resolution 452.

In fact, seeing it through a historical perspective, from 1996 until now, there are many "Nostradamus" elements. Many of the things that were written there have been realized after that period.

Now I'll speak about the Syrian side of it.

The "Clean Break" builds on the logic that since peace is harmful for Israel, harmful for the US, the best way is to look for problems beyond the crime scene: occupation. The first phase of it was in the Iraq war. In Iraq, they were publicly discussing for almost a full year that Iraq is a threat to the international stability and security, and with Iraq unable to do anything to prove that it was not a threat. With the end of the war, Iraq proved to be a non-threat. The initiators of the war believed that Saddam was wrong. Now the voices are appearing, are heard that the composition of Iraq is wrong.

During the Iraq war was the first mention of Syria. The accusations came once during a hearing in Congress that there should be a change in Syria. Second, the accusation that Syria was smuggling arms into Iraq, although Iraq was a threat, that Syria was smuggling arms into Iraq.

And the other accusation was that Iraq was smuggling arms into Syria; (by that) I mean weapons of mass destruction. This is what Sharon was saying. I mean a very strange, contradictory set of accusations. But then, anything you wanted, you got.

Syria was concerned and did its utmost to keep the situation under control. The region is very much unstable now. In the occupied territories, the Israeli-Palestinian issue, and in Iraq. And you can follow the terrorist attacks, which are going on in Mecca, Saudi Arabia, Turkey, and other places.

The strategy of Syria, in fact, has not changed. Syria is firmly committed to international diplomacy, and firmly believes in peace. It has called for peace in the Middle East since 1975 under the international auspices of the UN. This materialized in 1991 during the Madrid conference. We entered into negotiations with the Israelis and we almost resolved, under Rabin and Barak, about 80 percent of the issues. Maybe one of the good outcomes of the war in Iraq was that the "Clean Breakers" tended to refer to Iraq as not fulfilling about eighteen UN resolutions, to build international legitimacy.

Syrian rights are protected in thirty UN Security Council resolutions and about 500 General Assembly resolutions.

Syria enjoys good relations, regionally and internationally. Some of the "Clean Breakers," in fact, from the Congress, wrote a letter to the Administration in 1991 to block the

4. A Syrian Perspective: Peace is Dangerous for Israel

admission of Syria to the nonpermanent seat of the National Security Council, but Syria got about 170 votes. They wanted the Administration to oppose the will of 170 countries.

We have very good relations with the European Union; we are preparing for a partnership association agreement that might be signed by the end of this year. We have very good relations, in fact, with all Arab countries, and very good relations now with Turkey.

The elements of a "Clean Break" are not there. Whatever is said about the Syrian internal situation, we enjoy a very relaxed—I mean, economically slightly difficult, but a very relaxed internal situation. We enjoy stability and security. Everyone knows that about Syria. We don't have problems.

Some people are trying to promote now some kind of outside group and fabricate opposition elements. These opposition groups are a burden on the people who are trying to promote them and will prove to be that. Syria is a signatory to the Beirut peace initiative, the King Abdullah peace initiative for full relations, full peace for full withdrawals.

5
The Need for a "Clean Fix"

Entrepreneur and civic leader Dr. E. Faye Williams is an accomplished attorney, businesswoman, and teacher. She received her Ph.D. in Public Administration from City University of Los Angeles; Juris Doctorate, Howard University School of Law; Master's of Public Administration, University of Southern California. She is the author of three other books on political and foreign affairs, one of which is entitled The Peace Terrorists *and chronicles her 40-day peace mission leading up to the 1992 Gulf War. For 20 of those days, she and 200 women from around the world were held at gunpoint in the Arabian Sea off the coast of Oman in the Middle East. In 1995 she helped organize the Million Man March, serving as host committee co-chair and international spokesperson. At the march, Williams was one of the few women to address the large crowd assembled on the National Mall.*

I'm delighted to discuss a subject that has been troubling me for many years now. There was a time when we as Americans could trust our leaders; we could depend upon them to first and foremost do what is in the interest of the American people, without violating the rights of people around the world.

Now Richard Perle's study group document outlines a set of policies to be pursued in the Middle East, not only by Israel, but also by the United States, and if you've not read this document, let me just say that it is a chilling document.

For this group, not elected by anybody in the United States or Israel, or any country for that matter, to so brazenly plan the manipulation and the management of US leaders to comply

38

with policies the "Clean Break" group felt were in the best interest of all, regarding Syria and Lebanon and Turkey and Jordan and Palestine and many others. Now, if you don't do research, if you didn't analyze daily events, if you didn't listen carefully to the news and the other contradictions and then you didn't look for the other side, then you're not hearing these things from mainstream media. So you really have no way to "get it" except for the occasional brave, alternative voice that gives a view.

You wouldn't understand the impact of the Perle document that others have on determining US policy in the Middle East for Israel as well as the United States of America. And, of course, you know why, if you read this document, and you understand it, why we are becoming isolated in the world.

Now, have those policies brought peace and justice anywhere in the world? No they have not, and they won't. And you've heard the professor say many of the reasons they won't.

There was a time when Americans were welcomed everywhere around the world, I know. But, in essence, now we have been denied a fundamental right to travel because of the danger of identifying yourself as an American. Now when you analyze "Clean Break," you understand why this is so.

I don't believe the rest of the world belongs to some "axis of evil," as some of our leaders have pointed out. That is what I've seen them say, but I've not seen that as I've talked with people around the world, and I've criss-crossed this wonderful planet of ours. I don't believe that Cold War metaphors that "A Clean Break" suggests are relevant in today's complex international system. They were irrelevant the moment they were out there from this group.

I still believe in the basic goodness of the Iraqi people, the Palestinian people, the Muslims—almost all Muslims—and many of the Israelis that I've met around the world, whether they are in the US or abroad.

And I can express this belief because I know many of these people. I see them as human beings. I have traveled to their homes, I've spent time with them, I've been a guest in their homes, I've heard their cries and felt their spirit often—and they just want to be treated fairly. And they want peace. I mean, that's the normal thing to want.

Now, I know this, also because I am a Black American, and that's also what we as Black Americans want, and what we've had to fight for and to explain all of our lives. So I have an affinity with people who are being treated unfairly.

If you're in power, I know that it's difficult for you to understand what the lost, the least, and the left out want, because dissenting voices are rarely heard in our nation. We rarely have a platform to give those alternative, or as they're called, "alternative views."

I have faith that when the American people pause and think about what is happening to our world as a result of the policies and the obvious alignment of policies with those of a small group purporting to represent that nation—when the news people begin to think and begin to pause, they will too begin to challenge some of the things that they are just repeating right now. And the world, of course, will be better for that pausing and thinking.

In 1995, you've heard that I played a pivotal role in what was called the "Million Man March," bringing more than a million men to Washington, D.C. for peaceful purposes to speak for the often maligned Black man in this country, and rarely did we have mainstream media covering what we were doing, either before we got here or after the march was over, to capitalize on bringing that one million men together. Actually, the one million-plus men were already here in Washington, staring the media in their eyes, before they began to address or to show what was going on. They gave us little or no help.

Now, as a Black American, despite the consequences, I have often been compelled to speak out for people who cannot speak for themselves, whether they are here in the United States or whether they're abroad.

5. The Need for a 'Clean Fix'

And in these days of managed media, alternative voices have got to seek greater opportunities for the masses of the people to be heard. And about what the impact of this document, "A Clean Break," can have on us, as people who are not in the majority race in this country, but who are not in the minority around the world.

Now, for several years, some of us have had the audacity to speak out on a subject like Middle East policy, and of course, I dare say that we've been punished for it. Because somehow the Middle East is supposed to be an untouchable subject, except for those who are in power.

I have seen otherwise strong, honest, eloquent, powerful people just somehow cringe, and kow-tow, and become mum, in the subject of Middle East policy. They babble, they back down, you hardly know them as the same people on anything that might be perceived as critical or unflattering to Israel or to US policy in the Middle East. Even presidents find it difficult to speak out on this issue and to perform their duties. In 1991, after the first President Bush threatened to veto [Israel] loan guarantees as a foreign policy lever, he correctly quantified the wall of opposition that stifles all debate on this subject. And I'll quote what he said. He said there is "something like a thousand lobbyists on the Hill," and that may be an understatement, "to work the other side of the question...we've got one lonely little guy down here doing it."

Now since that time, the situation has gone downhill, if there is such a thing as going downhill from there.

Now, never mind the fact that many of Israel's high-ranking intelligence and military personnel have begun stepping forward to openly question Israeli policies and tactics toward Palestinians, as they use the word, "disgraceful." I applaud them for their courage. Our own Congress is quiet or they're defensive on this subject. Their cowardice is palpable here on the Hill. It is well known around the world. It is even beneath contempt. And apparently those who say that they care about young children are just kind of "out of it." They're not hearing. Their hearing has gone bad.

Having been fortunate enough to travel to Israel, having heard Israelis discuss the inhuman way in which Palestinians are treated by the Israelis in power, I have no doubt that it is safer to criticize Israel within its own borders than it is to criticize Israel here in our country.

Now, after carefully examining Richard Perle's document, and seeing how closely aligned it is with the Bush administration leaders who say and do many things, then I am more concerned than ever that US policy in the Middle East has gone seriously wrong. It has very little to do with protecting the world from terrorism or what is in the best interest of the United States, or in the best interest of our allies. Or the best interests of Israel, for that matter.

You see, I am a disciple of the Reverend Dr. Martin Luther King, and Dr. King once said, "There comes a time when we must speak out, there is a time when silence is betrayal." And I know the personal price that one can pay for speaking out on US policy in the Middle East, and yet it must be done.

More people must begin to speak out.

There are many others in our country who've been punished because they've had the audacity to simply question the billions of dollars that are spent on Israel annually. Many believe that a program of "tough love" that keeps family members from going astray would work in this relationship as well. Many Israelis believe that such massive aid distorts their own economy and damages their economy. Many of them have said it. Many of their leaders have said it. And of the few redeeming qualities of "A Clean Break"—and I say a few, because there are only a few—the call for economic reform and less reliance on aid is a positive thing in the document. Now, many of the same leaders here on Capitol Hill who continue to support a reckless and unconditional US policy in the Middle East have privately said to me, "I wish I had the courage you have."

5. The Need for a 'Clean Fix'

Well, to you I say this: "Tough love is true love. Unconditional support is a path toward disaster." And so we must begin to take a look at that.

If members of Congress have any doubts that they can fight the negative currents, I offer myself as a humble example that it is possible. After years of having my credentials and qualifications and certifications questioned, I've gone back to school, and you've heard all of the five or six, I lose track, terminal degrees that I've gotten or will be getting in the next few months—I just want you to see, those who are afraid, that I'm still standing, and I'm still fighting, and I'm going to continue to do it until we see a balanced Middle East policy.

Now, like many others who are horrified by the implications of the Perle document, "A Clean Break," I say to them, give me a break! It's not a "Clean Break" that's needed for bringing peace and justice to our world. It is a "Clean Fix."

Now, my mother told me, "Never bring problems to me without bringing some suggestions on how to resolve it." So let me see if I can do just a few. My recommendations are, first of all:

1.   To help our leaders to understand that where there is no justice, there will be no peace. The Palestinian people deserve the right to diplomatic recognition toward accelerated statehood now.

2.   Organize Americans to join in a coalition of conscience of millions of people around the world, of every race, creed, color, national origin, just as we worked together to get the Civil Rights Act, to get the Voting Rights Act, the Public Accommodations Act, Housing, and to get the Martin Luther King holiday. It was done then, it can be done again.

And this coalition is now led by former Congressman Walter Fauntroy, who has a long history of speaking out on human rights. And we find that true of many African-Americans in this country, because we understand. Damu Smith of Black Voices for Peace is on the right track. Gene Bird of Council for the National Interest is on the right track. Gerri Bird of

Partners for Peace, these are groups in which I am involved also, they are on the right track. Now, we must come together as one big group.

3.   We must register millions more people in this country, so that on Election Day they can go to the polls and they can hold people accountable who do not have the best interest of the United States at heart, but rather, they are more concerned about someone else and they are more concerned about a "clash of civilizations."

4.   We must reinstitute and increase cultural exchanges between our schools and our universities and schools and universities abroad; we must bring more Arab groups, we must bring more Arab staff, and even Israeli staff and others, and we must have these exchanges and have these discussions.

5.   We must speak out against our leaders who alienate us from the world by using technological and military superiority to dominate the world politically and economically, and who advance policies that have devastating effects on our lives and the lives of millions of people around the world.

6.   We must urge more people to come together; the elderly, the young, the rich, the poor, Asians, Hispanics, Arabs, Protestants, Catholics, Jews, it doesn't matter, Native Americans, we must come together.

These things, at a minimum, we must do if we ever want to see peace and justice. We must break the silence on US policy in the Middle East—more than a Million Man March is needed. We need more than 300 million people marching for peace and justice.

Having an outdated, bipolar, militaristic approach to resolving challenges is too costly and is also naïve. Also, the impact on Black Americans, of these policies, is much greater on us, more so because we have, I'm told, some 16-18 percent involved and dying in the military. (Note: Black Americans make up approximately 12.33 percent of the general population and 16.67 percent of the total 2002 Army, Navy,

5. The Need for a 'Clean Fix'

Marine, Coast Guard, and other reserve forces.) So it is more costly to us, but we would be concerned about anyone.

If Black America could lead a million men to Washington for peaceful purposes without mainstream media, then surely the administration has the ability to execute a sharp change in the course, to lead a million men and women and more, not to combat, but peacefully to do what should be accomplished through intelligent diplomacy.

Our ability to bring back diplomacy is limited by our inability to be heard—because the militaristic voices of Bush and Cheney and Rumsfeld, and Wolfowitz, and Bolton and Perle, are drowning out the rational voices.

With many voices speaking out for world peace and justice, we have a better opportunity to be heard and to make a difference.

I believe America both needs and wants to hear voices other than the ones we're hearing every day.

6
"Clean Break" with the Roadmap

William James Martin is a visiting professor at the University of Central Florida, Orlando. An analyst of neoconservative politicians in the US government, his work has been published in Counter Punch, Media Monitors, and other online journals.

Is there some difference in understanding and perspective between President George W. Bush and the members of his administration who are the dominant influences over foreign policy? Is the President, possibly because he is generally neither well-read nor well-informed, a relatively weak influence in his own administration that is dominated by such highly intelligent and forceful members of the Pentagon as Wolfowitz, Perle, Feith, and others, and by the Vice President? There is some evidence for this and some reason to believe it.

The following exchange took place at the Aqaba Summit on June 5, 2003 between Bush and Israeli Defense Minister Shaul Mofaz:

According to The Guardian, Palestinian Defense Minister Dahlan gave a five-minute synopsis of the Palestinian view of the security situation and the difficulties he faces because the Israelis have destroyed much of the Palestinian security infrastructure. At the end of the briefing, General Mofaz jumped in. "Well," he said, "they won't be getting any help from us; they have their own security service." Bush turned to General Mofaz. "Their own security service? But you have destroyed their security service," he reportedly said.

General Mofaz remained firm. "I do not think that we can help them, Mr. President," he said. Bush replied, "Oh, but I think that you can, and I think that you will." A similar confrontation followed with Sharon.

According to the Guardian story, towards the end of the summit, Bush told Condoleezza Rice, his national security

6. 'Clean Break' with the Roadmap

adviser, that he liked and trusted Abbas and Dahlan, but that Sharon was "a problem."

In July 2003, on the podium with then-Palestinian Prime Minister Mahmoud Abbas, President George W. Bush said: "It is very difficult to develop confidence between the Palestinians and the Israelis...with a wall snaking through the West Bank."

On Friday, December 12, 2003, President Bush urged Israel to avoid measures that could block a Palestinian state: "It's in Israel's interest there be a Palestinian state," Bush said, adding, "It's in the poor, suffering Palestinian people's interest there be a Palestinian state."

A few days later, US Deputy Assistant Secretary of State and Bush administration envoy to the Middle East David Satterfield said in Rome that Israel had "done too little for far too long" to foster peace negotiations with the PNA.

This exchange between Bush and Israeli Defense Minister Mofaz was striking in its singularity, for it was apparently the first time on record that there had been a sharp disagreement between Bush and the Sharon government in which Bush evidently understood the burden of the Palestinian Authority's providing for Israeli security with a police force and police installations largely destroyed by the Israeli army.

The December 12th statement expressed an understanding of the suffering of the Palestinians, an attitude rarely heard within the Bush administration.

If it is difficult to imagine these expressions from Bush, it is beyond imagination to picture them coming from civilian Pentagon officials, Wolfowitz, Perle, Douglas Feith, or David Wurmser at State, except possibly as a prelude to condemning Arafat.

But President Bush's irritation with Israel's "security" wall has not been translated into policy, as the US subsequently vetoed the UN Council Resolution declaring the construction of the wall to be in violation of international law. The US also joined Israel in opposing the legitimacy of any opinion rendered by the International Court of Justice meeting in the Hague in response to the Palestinian petition regarding the illegality of the wall.

Indeed, Perle, Wurmser, and Feith are on record as being committed to policies which are radically at variance with long-standing American policy and are also radically at variance with President Bush's roadmap.

At focus in this context is their document, "A Clean Break: A New Strategy for Securing the Realm," written in 1996 for the incoming Netanyahu government of Israel by Richard Perle, Douglas Feith, David and Meyrav Wurmser, James Colbert, and Robert Loewenberg in their capacity as members of the Institute for Advanced Strategic and Political Studies' "Study Group on a New Israeli Strategy Toward 2000," a Washington/Jerusalem-based think tank providing policy analyses for the government of Israel. This document is remarkable for its very existence, because it constitutes a policy manifesto for the Israeli government penned by members of the current US government. Richard Perle was, until his recent resignation, Chairman of the Defense Policy Board, and now continues to sit on the board. Douglas Feith is currently Undersecretary of Defense for Policy, the department's number three man, and a protégé of Perle who has worked closely with him in the past. David Wurmser is assistant to Undersecretary for Arms Control John Bolton at the State Department, the latter coming from the far right conservative American Enterprise Institute.

This document makes the following points:

1. "Israel has the opportunity to make a clean break; it can forge a peace process and strategy based on an entirely new intellectual foundation..."

2. The previous Israeli government's pursuit of a peace process, which was responsive to "supranational over national sovereignty... undermined the legitimacy of the nation and lead Israel to strategic paralysis." That peace process obscured

the evidence of an "eroding national critical mass—including a palpable sense of national exhaustion—and forfeited strategic initiative. The loss of national critical mass was illustrated best by Israel's efforts to draw in the United States to sell unpopular policies domestically, to agree to negotiate sovereignty over its capital...."

3. Israel should "work closely with Turkey and Jordan to contain, destabilize, and roll back some of its most dangerous threats. This implies clean break from the slogan 'comprehensive peace' to a traditional concept of strategy based on balance of power."

4. Israel should "change the nature of its relations with the Palestinians, including upholding the right of hot pursuit for self defense into all Palestinian areas and [should nurture] alternatives to Arafat's exclusive grip on Palestinian society."

5. "While previous governments, and many abroad, may emphasize "land for peace"—which placed Israel in the position of cultural, economic, political, diplomatic, and military retreat—the new government can promote Western values and traditions. Such an approach...includes 'peace for peace', 'peace through strength,' and self reliance: the 'balance of power.'"

6. "Displaying moral ambivalence between the effort to build a Jewish state and the desire to annihilate it by trading land for peace will not secure peace now. Our claim to the land—to which we have clung for hope for 2000 years—is legitimate and noble..."

7. "Only the unconditional acceptance by Arabs of our rights, especially in their territorial dimensions, 'peace for peace,' is a solid basis for the future. "

The breathtaking import of this program should not be obscured. The rejection of "land for peace," the identification of withdrawal from territory with "annihilation" of the state of Israel, and the pursuit of the "unconditional acceptance" of Israel's rights (apparently including the right to expand its borders) by the Arab states, constitute a radical departure from thirty-six years of American Middle East policy that embraces UN Resolution 242 and all subsequent Security Council Resolutions on the Middle East. It is also at radical variance with the roadmap, which embodies the two-state solution and calls for the establishment of a "viable and contiguous Palestinian state."

Under the subheading "Securing the Northern Border":

8. "Syria challenges Israel on Lebanese soil. "

9. Israel should engage Hezbollah, Syria, and Iran as the principal agents of aggression in Lebanon by striking Syrian military targets in Lebanon, and should that prove insufficient, striking at select targets in Syria proper.

10. "Given the nature of the regime in Damascus, it is natural and moral that Israel abandon the slogan 'comprehensive peace' and move to contain Syria... rejecting 'land for peace' deals on the Golan Heights. "

Under the subheading "Moving to a Traditional Balance of Power Strategy":

11. "Israel can shape its strategic environment, in cooperation with Turkey and Jordan by weakening, containing, and even rolling back Syria. "

12. "This effort can focus on removing Saddam Hussein from power in Iraq—an important strategic objective in its own right—as a means of foiling Syria's regional ambitions. "

13. "Damascus fears that a 'natural axis' with Israel on one side, central Iraq and Turkey on the other, and Jordan, in the center would squeeze and detach Syria from the Saudi Peninsula. For Syria, it would be a prelude to redrawing the map of the Middle East... "

14. Iraq's future could affect the strategic balance in the Middle East profoundly.

6. 'Clean Break' with the Roadmap

It is amazing how much of this program, though written for the Israeli government of Netanyahu of 1996, has already been implemented, not by the government of Israel, but by the Bush administration: the overthrow of Saddam Hussein in Iraq, the two-year-old house arrest of Arafat and the attempt to cultivate a new Palestinian leadership, the complete rejection by Sharon of the land-for-peace agreement on the Golan Heights with little US demurral, and the bombing inside of "Syria proper," with the only response from Bush being "Israel has a right to defend itself." In this complete rejection, de facto if not de jure, of the Roadmap, Sharon is well aware that he is supported by the Bush administration to such an extent that Bush himself can well be ignored.

After interviewing CIA officials including George Tenet, US diplomats, and Syrian President Bashar Assad, investigative journalist Seymour Hersh, writing in the *New Yorker* under the title "The Syrian Bet," has described how American officials burned a Syrian source of intelligence on Al Qaeda largely because of Syrian support for Hezbollah in southern Lebanon, and also because the government has allowed Hamas and the Palestinian Islamic Jihad to maintain offices in Damascus.

Because the secular Syrian government had been at war for more than two decades with the Syrian Muslim Brotherhood, based in Aleppo with close ties to Al Qaeda, Syria had compiled hundreds of files on Al Qaeda, including dossiers on the men who participated in the September 2001 attack on the World Trade Center and the Pentagon. Syria had also penetrated Al Qaeda cells throughout the Middle East and in Arab exile communities throughout Europe. Many of the airline hijackers of the September 2001 attack had operated out of cells in Hamburg and Aachen. Some members of these cells worked for a German firm called Tatex, which was infiltrated by Syrian intelligence during the eighties.

Hersh states that just after the September 2001 attacks, the Syrian government began allowing the CIA and FBI to operate in Aleppo, and on one occasion provided the US with advanced knowledge of an Al Qaeda plot to fly a glider loaded with explosives into a building at the US Navy's 5th Fleet headquarters in Bahrain. Syria also provided the US with advanced knowledge of a plot against an American target in Ottawa.

American intelligence and the State Department told Hersh that by 2002, Syria had become one of the most effective sources of intelligence and one of the most important allies in the fight against Al Qaeda. After the September 11 attacks, Syria provided a flood of information to American operatives, which only ended with the onset of the Iraq war.

With the invasion of Iraq came constant threats from Rumsfeld, Condoleezza Rice, and members of the Pentagon, along with accusations that Syria is harboring some of the Iraqi Baathist leadership as well as having stashed Iraq's weapons of mass destruction. It is a poorly kept secret that the neoconservatives of the Pentagon want to see the fall of the Syrian government and that it is their next target after Iraq.

In June 2003, the American army attacked several vehicles inside the Syrian border, killing about 80 people, and detained several members of Syrian security, who spent several days in interrogation. Evidently, Rumsfeld believed that this small caravan of cars was carrying Saddam Hussein or other high-ranking Iraqi officials to sanctuary in Syria. It turned out to be little more than people smuggling gasoline.

In early October, after a suicide bombing in Israel, two Israeli Air Force F16 fighter jets attacked a position 10 miles from Damascus, which Israel said was a terrorist training camp but which Islamic Jihad said had not been used for two years. In either case, the point was made. In Washington, a senior administration official said, "We have repeatedly told the government of Syria that it is on the wrong side in the war on terror and that it must stop harboring terrorists."

Given the constant threats to the Syrian government of Bashar Assad, son of the late President Hafez Assad, including attacks by both the United States and Israel inside Syrian territory, it is little wonder that intelligence on Al Qaeda provided by Syrian intelligence has ceased.

One sees, in the case of the Syrian relation, a conspicuous instance of Israeli interest eclipsing American interest. Al Qaeda, not Islamic Jihad or Hamas, is a threat to the United States. Islamic Jihad and Hamas threaten Israel, not the United States.

In February of 2002, the Saudi Crown Prince Abdullah advanced what became known as the Saudi Initiative, in which Arab states would offer normal diplomatic relations, including peace agreements that would recognize Israel's right to exist within secure borders, in return for Israel's withdrawal to its 1967 borders including withdrawal from East Jerusalem. When the Crown Prince was the guest of the President at his ranch near Crawford, Texas in April, he found that President Bush was barely aware of the plan and had not been briefed on it. Bush has said that he does not independently keep up with the news, but rather relies on his staff for briefings.

In fact, there is little motivation within the administration for briefing Mr. Bush on a proposal centered around the "land for peace" formula, which has been forthrightly rejected by the major foreign policy players of this administration.

The major players in foreign policy—Perle, Wolfowitz, Cheney, Feith, Wurmser—are not the only sources of action within the administration; there is Colin Powell, there is the President himself. But the authors of "A Clean Break" have had dramatic success in shaping foreign policy to fit their conceptualization.

The following conclusions can be drawn with considerable confidence:

1. Drivers of the American government's Middle East policy are delineated in the document "A Clean Break" and are only partially congruent with the attitudes of the President. Much of the program of this document has already become reality and has eclipsed President Bush's roadmap, which embodied a two-state solution.

2. The authors of "A Clean Break," those driving American policy, derive their concepts based on Israeli security and Israeli interests, so that American foreign policy under the Bush administration is primarily serving the interest of Israel and only secondarily that of the United States.

3. The invasion of Iraq for the purpose of overthrowing Saddam Hussein was undertaken in the interest of Israel, although it was paid for with American capital and American and Iraqi lives. David Kay, chief US weapons inspector in Iraq, has stated that Iraq almost certainly possessed no weapons of mass destruction on the eve of the American invasion; this destroys any justification for the claim that Iraq posed an immediate threat to the United States.

7
Clean Break or Dirty War?

Institute for Research: Middle Eastern Policy published the following as a policy brief on March 27, 2003.

Great changes are seldom achieved without a plan. The Israeli policy paper "A Clean Break: A New Strategy for Securing the Realm" (ACB) was authored by a group of policy advisors to Israel. Subsequently, nearly all members of this group ascended to influential policy-making positions within US government, media, and academic circles. Many of the ACB policies, such as toppling the government of Iraq, are now in full implementation and present new challenges to the global community. Others, such as the reform of Israel's economy, have been abysmal failures, but generate little visibility or impact outside of Israel. (See Exhibit 1,)

Exhibit #1 "Clean Break" Policy Implementation Score Card through March, 2003

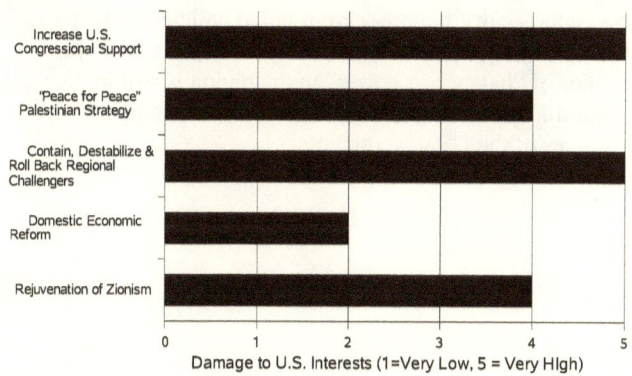

This chapter provides an overview of the policy implementation of "A Clean Break: A New Strategy for Securing the Realm" (full text is included in Appendix #1). Some of the events and trends that contribute to success or failure of the plan predate ACB by many years. And although many ACB authors ascended to new heights of political power in the US, the success or failure of the policies cannot be solely ascribed to them. However, ACB policies are, for the most part, extremely damaging to US interests. The ACB framework is useful for explaining the motives driving the complete failure of US interests in the Middle East and the triumph of politics and lobbies over statecraft.

Securing the Realm: Background

"A Clean Break: A New Strategy for Securing the Realm" (ACB) contains six pages of policy recommendations for Benjamin Netanyahu. In 1996, Israel's newly elected Prime Minister relied upon opinion makers, thinkers, and researchers to craft the paper. The Institute for Advanced Strategic and Political Studies' "Study Group on a New Israeli Strategy Toward 2000" included Richard Perle, James Colbert, Charles Fairbanks, Douglas Feith, Robert Loewenberg, David Wurmser, and Meyrav Wurmser.

The paper's call for a break from failed policies of the past, such as "land for peace," and a new concentration on the realities of "balance of power" in the region is striking for its realpolitik approach and high dependence on actions and resources of the US government.

7. Clean Break or Dirty War?

Exhibit #2 ACB Policy Initiatives

Increase US Congressional Support	"Electrify and find support" of key US congressional members
	Strategic cooperation with US on missile defense
	Gain more support among members of Congress with little knowledge of Israel
	Harness support to move the US embassy to Jerusalem from Tel Aviv
	Identify Israel with the US and "Western values"
	Utilize Cold War rhetoric to make Israel's case to the American people
"Peace for Peace" Palestinian Solution	Eliminate movements toward a "comprehensive peace" and substitute with the "Peace for Peace" strategy
	Stress "balance of power" as sole test of legitimacy, enforce agreements
	Nurture alternatives to Arafat
	Seek legitimization of "hot pursuit" of Palestinian militants
	Eliminate "land for peace" concept, use negotiations only as a forum for communicating resolve
	Establish a joint monitoring committee with the US for measuring Palestinian compliance
	Withhold US aid to Palestinians
	Promote human rights among Arabs to isolate Palestinians in Arab constituencies
	Legitimize "2000-year-old historical land claims"
	Foment Arab recognition of Israel in exchange for peace

Neocon Middle East Policy

Contain, Destabilize, and Roll Back Regional Challengers	Challenge Arab countries as "police states" lacking in legitimacy.
	Fortify regional alliances, work with Turkey and Jordan to insert hostile Arab tribes into Syria
Syria	Publicly question Syrian legitimacy, assume treaties with Damascus are in bad faith
	Contain Syria, strike select targets
	Reject "land for peace" concept on the Golan Heights
Iraq	Install a Hashemite monarchy in Iraq
	Isolate and surround Syria with a friendly regime in Iraq
Lebanon	Engage Syria, Iran, and Iraq in Lebanon
	"Wean" Lebanese Shiites from Iraq toward Jordan
Economic Reform	Eliminate Social Zionism from the economy.
	Reform the overall economy, cut taxes
	Show maturity and economic self-reliance from the United States
	Eliminate need for defense by US military forces
	Remove US aid leverage over Israel
	Relegislate a free trade zone, sell off public lands and enterprises
Zionism	Rebuild Zionism, rejuvenate the national ideal
	"Shape the regional environment" in favor of Israel, "transcend foes" rather than contain them
	Pre-emption as the preferred national defense strategy

7. Clean Break or Dirty War?

Although ACB readers can identify nearly 34 distinct and actionable goals eloquently stated within the document, they may be summarized in five overarching policy goals:

1. Increase US Congressional Support

2. "Peace for Peace" Palestinian Strategy

3. Contain, Destabilize, and Roll Back Regional Challengers

4. Economic Reform

5. Rejuvenation of Zionism

In this paper, we evaluate the levels of implementation of these five summary goals and their effect on the interests of the United States. No set of policies ever comes to fruition without an active and vocal distribution and implementation network. ACB's legions of American shock troops are many. At its core, key operatives working within the Bush administration (called the neocons), policy research think tanks, specialty press, and opinion columns have achieved amazing success at molding ACB policy agenda items into "vital interests" of the United States itself. (See Exhibit 3.)

Crime-scene levels of evidence linking ACB followers to the actions of the US government at Israel's behest are unnecessary. Many US actions are simply so inexplicable that consideration of their chief benefactor, Israel, is the only reasonable explanation. And while Americans dismiss Arab government charges that Israel is attacking them by proxy across the region, the evidence shows that the Arabs are correct. "A Clean Break" is, at heart, a proclamation of "Dirty War."

Exhibit #3 The Neocon Policy Distribution and Implementation Network

Groups	Messages	Medium	Members
Defense	Preemption/ remaking the Middle East Aid for Israel/joint weapons development New Homeland Security business opportunities Legitimization of Israeli occupation of Palestinian territories	Think tanks Defense Policy Board Defense Department Defense contractors Talk shows Investment banks	Paul Wolfowitz Richard Perle Douglas Feith Elliot Abrams David Wurmser
Neocon Specialty Press	Danger of Islam Illegitimacy of all Arab governments Illegitimacy of "land for peace" initiatives Primacy of the defense of Israel	American Enterprise Institute, JINSA, and Heritage Foundation reports The Weekly Standard The New Republic commentary (American Jewish Committee)	David Brooks Lawrence Kapla William Kristol Norman Podhore
Columnists/Pundits	Palestinian militants as "terrorists" Linkage between 9/11 and all Arab governments Israelis as "heroes" Critics of Israel as "anti-Semites"	Wall Street Journal New York Times Washington Post editorial pages	Robert Kagan Charles Krauthammer Max Boot William Safire

Core members of the group have been able to raise the primacy of Israeli issues to a level that Americans would find absurd if the group were promoting the interests of any other state (such as Italy or Mexico). Their level of vitriol, hubris, and warmongering by the power of the pen and influence over American policy has been stunning. Many have personally engaged in activities that derailed official US foreign policy initiatives in the interest of improving Israel's power. Others have systematically chipped away at the US Constitution by supplanting Israeli interests for legitimate US interests in the Defense Department and the executive branch of the US government.

The gaping divide that separates this group's lobbying on behalf of Israel and the true interests of the United States also defines this group with the very label they so frequently hurl at others: traitors to the United States of America.

ACB Implementation Assessment

The levels of implementation of ACB policy objectives are not uniform; neither are the resources, Israeli and American, which have been rallied and deployed in their support. In this section, we consider the level of implementation success of each ACB policy summary.

a. Increase Support in the US Congress

It is political suicide for a member of the US Congress to strongly oppose policy positions of Zionist lobbies operating in the United States. Former President George H. W. Bush put it best when he declared that opposing the Zionist lobby in favor of a Palestinian state was the right thing to do, but came "at a hell of a price."

The defining demonstration of this power predates ACB. The lobby converted its most powerful aid opponent by rallying massive campaign contributions toward defeating North Carolina senator Jesse Helms. Pro-Israel political action committees poured an awe-inspiring $222,342 into the campaign of Helms' opponent, North Carolina Governor James Hunt. Hunt's campaign secretary proclaimed that "Senator Helms has the worst anti-Israel record in the United States Senate and supporters of Israel throughout the country know it."

After the scare of almost losing reelection, Helms announced that he would exempt US foreign aid going to Israel from budget cuts, since such aid was "in the strategic interest of the US." He also became an ardent supporter of moving the US embassy from Tel Aviv to Jerusalem, and worked diligently to increase appropriations for Israel from the Defense Department, the State Department, and half a dozen other federal agency budgets.

A survey of recently introduced legislation indicates that Congress is repaying the debt to Israel by internalizing Israel's conflicts and putting US resources at Israel's disposal. (See Exhibit 4.)

Exhibit #4 Recent Pro-Israel Legislation Introduced in the US Congress

Legislation	Summary	Analysis
Koby Mandell Act of 2003	To create an office within the Department of Justice to undertake specific steps to ensure that all American citizens harmed by terrorism overseas receive equal treatment by the United States government regardless of the terrorists' country of origin or residence, and to ensure that all terrorists involved in such attacks are pursued, prosecuted, and punished with equal vigor, regardless of the terrorists' country of origin or residence.	Demonize the Palestinian Authority by labeling dual-citizen Israeli deaths in the ongoing Israeli-Palestinian conflict as "acts of terrorism" that the US Department of Justice can pursue. Understandably, the legislation does not address the summary arrest and torture of Arab-American citizens by the Israeli Shin-Bet.
H.RES.61 Whereas the United States and Israel are close allies whose people share a deep and abiding friendship based on a shared commitment to democratic values	Commends the people of Israel for conducting free and fair elections, reaffirming the friendship between the Governments and peoples of the United States and Israel, and for other purposes.	Seeks to coerce the Palestinian leadership to censor official media in opposition to Israel and take responsibility for the security of Israel by controlling many radical groups essentially beyond its control.
HR 167 IH	To take certain steps toward recognition by the United States of Jerusalem as the capital of Israel.	Seeks to create another set of "facts on the ground" by eliminating resistance to moving US diplomatic facilities to the contested city of Jerusalem from Tel Aviv. Also seeks recognition of births in Jerusalem as being births in Israel and identification in all US government documents of Jerusalem as the capital in spite of international opposition to legitimizing the issue.

HR 1358 IH International School Curriculum Monitoring Act (Introduced in House)	Seeks to monitor all international curriculums for "anti-Semitic" material and tie US aid to official US approval of such educational material.	Would codify McCarthy-type independent monitoring groups tied to Zionist organizations such as Daniel Pipe's infamous "Campus Watch." Legitimizes yet another lever for Israeli operatives to influence and deny aid to countries that legitimately oppose Israel.
SCON 32 IS Senator Lindsey Graham and Congressman Joe Wilson Resolution to protect and open up all holy sites in the state of Israel and nearby territory	Expresses the sense of Congress regarding the protection of religious sites and the freedom of access and worship in the state of Israel and "nearby territories." The resolution states that the holy sites currently under the sovereignty of the state of Israel should remain under Israeli protection and that all holy sites in the region remain open to visitors of all faiths.	Seeks to solidify 1967 borders and Israeli occupied territories by putting their religious sites under Congressionally legitimized protection mirroring Israel's "Israeli Protection of Holy Places Law of 1967," which states that freedom of access and worship is ensured at all places of worship and religious significance.

Most of the legislation is costly to the United States in constraining American civil liberties and foreign policy initiatives in the Middle East while legitimizing even the most despicable Israeli actions that much of the rest of the world community consider to be crimes. These gestures create enmity with nations and states with which the US should have steadily improving relationships. As an ACB policy goal, IRmep applies a score of 5 out of 5 to demonstrated Israeli influence over the US Congress.

b. "Peace for Peace" Approach to the Palestinian Question

Israel has adopted all of the appearances of promoting a "peace for peace" strategy with the Palestinians. Under this policy, Palestinians have no land claims on territory within the borders of Israel or territory occupied by Israel. Palestinians and future "enemies" under this policy must be content only with avoiding their own destruction by Israel.

7. Clean Break or Dirty War?

One aggressive approach promoted by Richard Perle, former chairman of the US Defense Policy Board, labels Jordan as Palestine, implying relocation or "ethnic cleansing" of Palestinian peoples. "Land for Peace" as a strategy is widely discredited by pro-Israel agents as unworkable and lacking in security for Israel. Current efforts to derail remnants of "Land for Peace" include:

1. Israeli Security Time Limits
On March 31, 2003, Israeli Foreign Minister Silvan Shalom indicated that Israel will only give the Palestinian Prime Minister-designate two months to crack down on terrorism. By placing the Prime Minister in charge of Israeli security against forces entirely outside his circle of influence, Israel creates ideal conditions for rejecting land-for-peace movements while accelerating settlement activity.

2. Legitimizing Israeli Delays through Amendments to the Roadmap
The roadmap for peace proposed by the European Union, Russia, the United Nations, and the United States was originally designed to be non-negotiable for both Israel and Palestine. Intense lobbying pressure has produced cracks that open the possibility for endless Israeli negotiations and delays of the roadmap, as Israel proposes 12 major changes to this seven-page document. On March 14, 2003, President Bush gave Israel license to pursue the amendment strategy in a Rose Garden announcement. "The United States has developed this plan over the last several months in close cooperation with Russia, the European Union, and the United Nations. Once this roadmap is delivered, we will expect and welcome contributions from Israel and the Palestinians to this document that will advance true peace."

3. Discrediting Roadmap Architects
Prime Minister Ariel Sharon and network members have worked diligently to discredit roadmap architects, particularly European nations. While Israel was unsuccessful in blocking some conferences and Palestinian contributions to the roadmap, the current political climate in the US after traditional allies and the UN failed to support the US invasion

of Iraq has boosted Israel's chances of creating schisms in the quartet.

Because Israel has not yet been able to completely derail the roadmap, IRmep assigns a score of only 3 out of 5 for promotion of the "peace for peace" strategy.

c. Contain, Destabilize, and Roll Back Regional Challengers

The US invasion of Iraq is such a singular success for Israel that pro-Israel leaders and pundits in the United States have had to restrain their glee; a long and arduous effort to topple Iraq's government and neutralize the state has finally borne fruit.

Although Iraq is only one challenger to Israel, an accelerated Israeli effort to discredit, disrupt, and undermine other Arab governments, many in the midst of democratic reform, is moving forward rapidly.

Exhibit #5 "Clean Break" Containment and Destabilization Policy Implementation

Target	Tactic	Result
Syria	**Threats of Invasion** In Secretary of State Colin Powell's speech to a conference of AIPAC members, he spoke of the "critical choice" facing Damascus. "Syria can continue to direct support for terrorist groups and the dying regime of Saddam Hussein, or it can embark on a different and more hopeful course. Either way, Syria bears the responsibility for its choices, and the consequences," he declared to loud applause.	The redirection of US forces to Syria after toppling Saddam Hussein is a high priority for Israel. An increase in allegations of Syrian transshipments of war materiel and use as an entry point for regional Muslims answering a call for Jihad could quickly be hyped into support for use of force by the massive US military force already in the region.
Syria	**Simmering Conflict** Violence in and around Golan Heights has flared. Hezbollah guerrillas on the border zone, who have been fighting to force the Israelis to withdraw, have killed seven Israeli soldiers.	Israel responded with air strikes that destroyed three Lebanese power stations and injured 20 civilians. Israel has continued its campaign to label all branches of Hezbollah as terrorists.
Iran	**Linking Freelancers to Iran** Defense Secretary Rumsfeld accused hundreds of Iraqi Shiite militia fighters based in Iran have crossed back into Iraq, complicating the military mission for the US-led coalition seeking to oust Iraqi leader Saddam Hussein. He has rushed to classify them as "combatants" even though the forces could be channeled onto the American side. Undersecretary of State John Bolton, a leading hawk, was quoted last month as telling Israeli officials that Iran would be "dealt with" after the war with Iraq.	By immediately rejecting the possibility of Shiite militia as allies and moving quickly to implicate the government of Iran for what are probably freelance operatives, the Bush administration advances another step down the ACB regional challenger path. Although the UK has rejected any support for Syrian and Iranian fronts, the mass of US forces could be immediately redeployed to attack Iran.
Saudi Arabia	**Smear and Defame** Former Defense Policy board Chairman Richard Perle spearheaded an	Perle contracted Rand Corporation analyst Laurent Muraweic on July 10, 2002.

	intense smear campaign against Saudi Arabia at the Pentagon, laying the foundations for future US military action.	RAND's briefing declared Saudi Arabia an "enemy of the United States" and advocated that the US invade the country, seize its oil fields, and confiscate its financial assets unless the Saudis "stop supporting the anti-Western terror network."
Egypt	**Conditioning and Cutting Foreign Aid** Condition aid to Egypt on increased support for Israel.	Legislation to engage in social engineering in Egypt by tying US foreign aid to rewriting curriculum to proselytize a better image of Israel. Media watch campaigns and scoring are also conditions of aid.

IRmep assigns an overall score of 4 out of 5 to Israeli efforts to destabilize and roll back regional rivals. While large successes have been scored in Iraq and Saudi Arabia, it is not yet clear that Israel will be able to motivate the US into armed conflict with Syria and Iran. Also, it is increasingly apparent that Arab nations are aware of the architects of Middle Eastern conflict and are strategizing to both expose and resist ACB proxy activities.

d. **Economic Reform**

Israel's efforts at economic reform have not yielded positive results. Although ACB calls for increased economic independence from the US, which would allow freer reign for Israeli policies that the US directly opposes, efforts at reform have been too little, too late. Israel has mismanaged its economy and continues to export the negative consequences to the United States.

7. Clean Break or Dirty War?

1. Israeli Economic Mismanagement

Hitting 103 percent of GDP in 2002, Israel maintains one of the highest government debt ratios in the world—a higher debt-to–GDP ratio than most OECD countries, surpassing that of Canada. The Bank of Israel predicts the ratio will balloon to at least 106 percent in 2003. Interest payments on the government debt, under international standards, amount to 8.1 percent of GDP, while the OECD average is 2.2 percent. This is unfavorable compared with 3.1 percent in Germany, 2.8 percent in France, 2 percent in the US, and 1.2 percent in Japan. The Bank of Israel believes that this continued and uncontrolled increase in interest payments on the government debt will reduce the government's ability to maintain infrastructure investments and social needs or freely set budget priorities. These interest payments on the government debt increased to NIS 39.5 billion in 2002, a fifth of the state budget. Economic mismanagement has caused the harshest recession in the country's 55-year history and two years of negative growth. Israel's gross domestic product dropped 1.1 percent in 2002, with unemployment at an average of 10.3 percent. The government ran up a $579 million budget deficit in February, the highest 30-day overdraft on record.

2. Eliminate Social Zionism

The kibbutz movement in Israel is symbolic of social Zionism, and it is in crisis. Only limited kibbutzim in Israel, numbering between 35 and 50, are doing well Though 2 percent of Israel's 6.2 million people live on kibbutzim, they generate 40 percent of the nation's agricultural produce and 10 percent of its industrial output. As Israel's youth flee the kibbutzim, the average age of members has spiraled upward. Communal financial capabilities for covering retirement and healthcare benefits are on life support, as Israelis come to realize the fundamental flaw in social Zionism. As one immigrant stated, "Our basic premise was wrong...The basic idea was that if we bring up our children in a non-competitive society, they would naturally want to live that way. . . That was a big mistake."

3. Overdevelopment/Reliance on High Tech

During the tech boom, Israel over developed its high-tech sector. Investments were made in spite of the lack of a supporting community of universities and high-tech educational facilities and domestic technology demand. Israel counted on being able to leverage preferential access to the US market for military and software products without taking into consideration the high competition with US and other global firms. The dramatic collapse of the Israeli high-tech sector also revealed the disproportionate effect that over-reliance on a volatile sector can have on a small country, as opposed to larger economies in Europe and the United States that have more successfully weathered the storm.

IRmep's assessment of economic reform in Israel is that it is much too little, much too late, leading to an ACB score of 1 out of 5. Perhaps this can be attributed to ACB's architects. While most are highly capable in securing foreign aid and political support for Israel, none were notable economists. The architects and their network, of course, lay much of the blame for Israel's economic malaise on Palestinian resistance to occupation.

e. **Rejuvenation of Zionism**

Zionism, defined as the international movement for the establishment of a Jewish national or religious community in Palestine and later for the support of modern Israel, is enjoying resurgence, though from unexpected quarters:

1. American Christian Zionist Movement

Support for Israel by organized Christian groups in the US has undergone explosive growth. Israel has been promoted and accepted as a cause that represents concrete steps toward the fulfillment of scriptural prophecy. One group, the two-million-member Christian Coalition, is able to quickly deploy voting guides to over 70 million US households for such causes as the legislative effort to solidify Israel's 1967 borders and occupied territories purely in the name of "protection of religious site access." The return of the Jews to their ancient homeland is seen by Evangelicals as a precondition for the mystical Second Coming of Christ. Therefore, when the Jewish state was created in 1948, evangelicals saw it as a sign. Israel's conquest of Jerusalem and the West Bank in 1967 deepened their excitement and multiplied their organized support for Israel.

2. Weakened International Opposition to Zionism

Twenty-six years ago, the United Nations General Assembly adopted a contentious resolution equating Zionism with racism. Then, as now, Israel mustered the support of the United States (and few other states) to stand by Israel's rejection of the resolution. Although conferences addressing the tie between Zionism and racism are again questioning Israel and the high Palestinian casualties produced by endless conflict, the US has been instrumental in stifling debate through its conspicuous absence at most human rights conferences.

3. More Effective Deployment of the "Anti-Semitism" Smear Attack

Critics of Israel in the major broadcast or print media are few in number. In 1919, Morris Jastrow, Jr. wrote the book *Zionism and the Future of Palestine*, published by the Macmillan Company. Jastrow correctly predicted that the intertwining of religion and nationality "political Zionism" would have negative consequences. He posited that whereas non-Jews have only one country and one purported loyalty ("Americans are American," " the French are French," etc.), Jews are seen as having split loyalties. He believed that they are both citizens of the country in which they live and also supporters of the Jewish state. He worried that Jews living outside Israel (occupied Palestine) would be seen as less than totally loyal to the countries where they reside. Right or wrong, Jastrow predicted that this political difference would add to real anti-Semitism. However, Jastrow failed to predict how effectively smear campaigns would be deployed by

Zionist entities such as the Anti-Defamation League when small numbers of agents of Israel were actually caught engaging in "activities incompatible with their status as American citizens." The suggestion by Pat Buchanan and other deeply conservative thinkers that "war party" members with undeniably compromising ties to Israel were the primary architects of the US invasion of Iraq have been met with a stifling wall of media rebukes and charges of anti-Semitism. However, though most potential critics of Israel in the mainstream media continue to be effectively muzzled, the charges and evidence are beginning to circulate beyond small groups of intellectuals and patriots.

One religion enjoys no protection. Across the dial of Christian Radio in Bible Belt America, listeners can hear shrill condemnations of Islam and testimony to the ascendancy and righteousness of Christian and Zionist principles acting in alliance against Islam.

High-profile conferences feature sessions by intellectual ideologues such as Daniel Pipes speaking about militant Islam and 15 percent of Muslims as potential terrorists have fanned xenophobia while Jerry Falwell proclaims that the prophet Mohammed himself was a terrorist. Countless millions of Americans are reading a series of novels called "Left Behind." They are topping bestseller lists all over the country and being made into movies. These books glorify and chronicle apocalyptic times. The setting is the twenty-first century, complete with war planes and TV correspondents.

This Christian fervor for the advance of Israel gives pause to many Jewish leaders. While these Christians believe that God gave the land of Israel to the Jewish people and that every grain of sand between the Dead Sea, the Jordan River, and the Mediterranean Sea belongs to the Jews, including the West Bank and Gaza, problems exist. The biblical version of the apocalypse either kills off Jews or has them converted to Christianity, making evangelical support a double-edged sword that is a poor guide to real geopolitics played out in the

Middle East on the ground. In the words of one clever observer, it "cuts us out in the fourth act."

And what biblical guidance is there for the three million Palestinians who live on the West Bank and Gaza? Some fundamentalists suggest the bulk of them should be cleansed from this God-given real estate and moved to another Arab country. In fact, many evangelicals believe that when Prime Minister Rabin signed the Oslo accords and offered to trade land for peace, it was not only a mistake, it was a sin that he paid for with his own life.

IRmep assigns a score of 5 to the ACB plan to rejuvenate Zionism. The effectiveness of the machinery in place to promote Zionism is awe-inspiring, although it comes from unexpected and, at times, wholly unwanted quarters.

ACB American Interest Damage Assessment

ACB represents a plan for achieving the best possible outcome for Israel. However, the policies that create a favorable outcome for Israel create an equal and opposite negative outcome for the United States. In this section, we analyze the extent of the damage and assign it a negative numerical score.

a. Increase US Congressional Support

The verifiable Israeli influence over the US Congress that indirectly emanates from different interest groups and lobbying organizations is tremendously damaging for the United States. As ideologues promote policies based on Israeli, Zionist, or even biblical objectives that are effectively enforced by US law and military might, portions of the American ideal begin to wither, die, and finally decay.

The first to go is the idea that the United States operates best as a secular entity. The Bill of Rights states, "Congress shall make no law respecting an establishment of religion." By accepting and exporting US power in support of the aims of two religions, Christianity and Judaism, Congress has violated the US Constitution and itself.

Smaller acts, such as distributing communications to US soldiers fighting in Muslim lands exhorting that they "pray for President Bush," are further disturbing signs that the United States' separation of church and state has been eroded to the point of collapse.

IRmep rates the damage assessment score for the increase in US Congressional Support at the very highest level, 5 out of 5.

b. "Peace for Peace" Palestinian Strategy

The collapse of the Oslo Accords and the degradation caused by the Israel Palestinian conflict have left only one party that can effectively enforce solutions to the crisis—the United States.

US interests in achieving peace in the region are of high importance. The conflict is seen as the linchpin of grievances throughout the Arab world. By siding with the interests of Israel and compromising its role as a neutral broker, the US has compromised its own legitimacy.

The chief US interest in the Middle East is promoting gradual and nonviolent political, social, and economic development of the entire region. Favoring only one country makes conflict in vital oil-producing regions more likely, motivates militant fundamentalist terrorist networks to act against the US, and strains US relations with the global community.

IRmep scores US adherence to a "peace for peace" rather than "land for peace" strategy as having a high level of damage to US Middle East interests: 4 out of 5.

c. Contain, Destabilize, and Roll Back Regional Challengers

The Israeli-motivated plan to "destabilize" and "redraw the map of the Middle East" may be remembered by future generations as the spark that fell into the tinder box of World War III. While the United States is clearly interested in the reform of governments and institutions across the Middle East, a slower and more gradual approach with less bloodshed was clearly the preferable path.

By accelerating conflict and casting aside international laws and alliances in the name of regime change, the US is increasingly perceived as a rogue state and every bit as much a UN pariah as Israel.

By picking fights with ethnicities and tribes about which it knows or chooses to know comparatively little, the Bush administration is only beginning to harvest the consequences of its ill-advised and ideologically motivated extremism.

IRmep's US damage assessment score is a solid 5 out of 5.

d. **Economic Reform**

Israel's economic reform has little direct effect on US interests. Although Israelis would like to further integrate economies, particularly in the military-industrial arena, the US frequently finds that this leads to unintended technology transfers. Israel's attempted sales of radar systems based on US AWACs and the Lavi fighter jet copied from the US F-16 platforms are strategically significant, damaging matters.

The continued dependence of Israel on US aid is a negative factor for the United States. The IRmep damage score to US interests is material. Ballooning aid to Israel, while minor as a percentage of total US GDP, alienates the global community and Arab states, since it is the highest single disbursement in the entire US foreign aid budget, at extremely favorable terms (equivalent to cash).

This is not good for Israel, and in spite of the boon to US arms manufacturers and defense contractor interests written into aid packages, it is negative for the US.

IRmep's US damage assessment score is 2 out of 5.

e. **Rejuvenation of Zionism**

Supporting the rejuvenation of Zionism has had a polarizing effect within the United States and has damaged the constitutionally protected freedoms of US citizens. As a case study, consider how two ideologically and religiously motivated soldiers departing for different destination countries are now treated by the US government.

An ardent and fit Jewish youth with American citizenship can easily travel to Israel and serve in the Israeli Defense Force or another government branch for two years, then return to blend back into US society. His activities, pledges of allegiance (which nullify US citizenship), and details of military service are of no interest to the US government. He could engage in two years of paramilitary operations against US Arab allies, or could return to the US with an ongoing intelligence liaison to Mossad; none of this will be questioned or investigated in the US.

An ardent and fit Palestinian youth with American citizenship departing for the West Bank faces different treatment. If he is in the minority of ardently religious Muslim Palestinians, he faces the wrath of both Israel and the US. He can be detained and imprisoned in Israel if authorities suspect any sympathy or support for Palestinian causes. US counsel in Tel Aviv will not provide support or US representation if the detainment ever reaches a judicial forum, which it may not.

If the Palestinian youth joins any group considered to be in militant opposition to Israel (though usually not the United States), he will implicate himself immediately in crimes of association with "terrorist" organizations and may be subject to detainment as an enemy combatant in Guantanamo Bay or even execution by US intelligence operatives. Militant opposition to Israel has been completely criminalized in the United States, and Israel itself publicly reserves the right to assassinate American citizens, in the United States, who are suspected of acting against the interests of Israel.

As a party to the promotion of Zionist activities over other religiously motivated military activities, the US has subtly codified military and other support of religion in a way that strikes at the very foundations on which it was formed.

7. Clean Break or Dirty War?

By selectively codifying support for Zionism, the US has set itself upon the course of intolerance and large-scale bloodshed. The damage to its reputation as a just, fair, and secular nation has been preempted by coalitions of evangelical interest groups and agents of Israel. IRmep's US damage assessment score is 4 out of 5. Practically speaking, US policies are becoming indistinguishable from an institutionalized modern crusade against Islam and Arab nations.

Conclusions

That ACB has realized high levels of implementation is undeniable. However, IRmep believes that the costs in terms of damage done to US foreign policy objectives and national interests are extremely high.

Exhibit #6 "Clean Break" Policy Implementation vs. US Damage Assessment Score Card

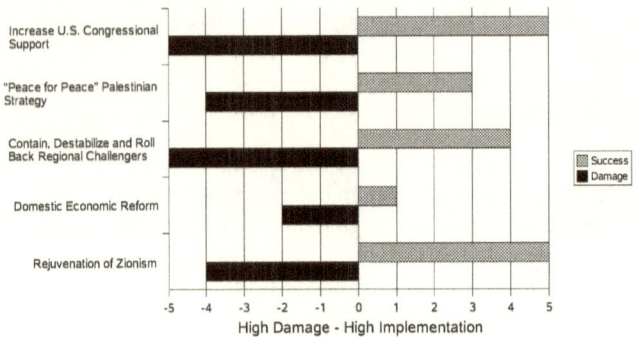

Though some damage may be irreparable, IRmep calls for US policy makers to immediately reconsider the costs of further ACB implementation. Following ACB can only generate additional damage to US interests in the future.

8
Rule of Law and Neocon Policy

Institute for Research: Middle Eastern Policy brief published 9/1/2004.

American Values vs. US Middle East Policy

The year 2004 plumbed dark new depths of America's foreign policies in the Middle East.   American citizens, who are usually willing to support official rationales for foreign policy, including military intervention, based on trust in the office of the President, now overwhelmingly oppose the US invasion of Iraq. 56 percent of respondents to a Washington Post-ABC News poll released on December 21, 2004 conclude that the conflict was not worth the fight, given mounting costs and new information that fundamental justifications for the invasion were incorrect. This new distrust is the backlash to a continuing series of legally and morally questionable actions that have stripped away America's former reputation as a country operating under the rule of law. (See Exhibit 1.)

Exhibit 1: US Departures from Rule of Law in Middle East Policy

Event	Analysis	Impact
"Clean Break" authors set precedent that front-running US policy is acceptable	Clean Breakers effectively "front-run" US policy and advise a foreign government to thwart US attempts to broker a Middle East peace.	An "anything goes" environment for US policy making and foreign elements in the Pentagon, White House, and Washington think tank community.
Abu Ghraib and Guantanamo torture scandals	Authorized use of "stress positions," attack dogs, and environment for sexual humiliation provide a new and startling image of the modus operandi of American military and intelligence forces in the region.	Future generations of US operatives in the Middle East will face populations who equate US armed forces with torture and sexual perversion, a vast departure from their reputation in other regions.
US torture memo [1]	The public release of a 2003 Pentagon policy paper outlining "legalisms" to sidestep Geneva Conventions and authorize US use of torture fosters a "might makes right, anything goes" attitude in US special ops, intelligence, and contractor communities.	The release of this memo ignites global perceptions that the US no longer abides by the Geneva Conventions and that the military believes the President has virtually unlimited powers to approve practices outlawed by international treaties.
WMD Iraq invasion rationale/false evidence	Deputy US Secretary of Defense Paul Wolfowitz made a public admission that WMD was merely one factor to overcome "bureaucratic" objections to war, and that WMD had never been the most compelling justification for invading Iraq.	Allies and opponents alike understand that the US is willing to employ false rationales to present the case for the most important decision a nation ever makes: whether or not to initiate a military conflict.
Iraqi debt influence peddling [2]	Carlyle Group and Albright Group, headed by luminaries James Baker and Madeline Albright, offer to shelter Kuwait's sovereign debt from official US efforts to renegotiate/eliminate outstanding Iraqi sovereign debt.	A January 2004 proposal to Kuwait made by Carlyle and Albright offers to protect Kuwaiti debt from US calls for debt forgiveness. Places special debt envoy Baker and former Sec. of State Albright in the position of lobbying against US interests on behalf of a foreign government in exchange for a $1 billion investment and potential management fees.

8. Rule of Law and Neocon Policy

Observers in the United States and abroad are coming to see the US as a force oblivious to truth, justice, and transparency, and not bound by the rule of law. In the Middle East, actors are forced by the evidence to conclude that the rule of law takes second place to the principle that "might makes right."

Analysts in the United States, as well as President Bush, have long trumpeted that Arabs, particularly Muslims, "hate us for our freedoms." Statistically relevant surveys in the region quickly dispense with this theory. According to the Zogby International Poll results released in June 2004, the Arab and Muslim population's favorable opinion of the US declines as a direct result of America's regional policy.

Exhibit 2: Favorable Opinion of the United States April 2002, June 2004

(Source: Zogby International)

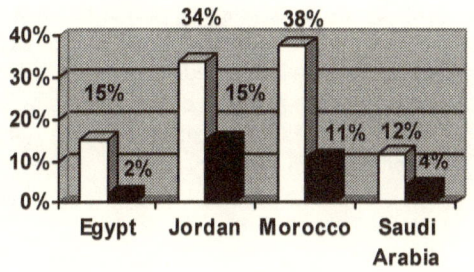

Regional opinion about the US is deteriorating because of "facts on the ground" transmitted via non-stop satellite coverage of the US military operations in Iraq and US-supported Israeli military actions in Palestine. The loss of moral high ground comes at the worst possible moment for US policymakers. American objectives to reverse nuclear proliferation and terrorism emanating from the region will fail if the rule of law is relegated to the dustbin. America can only succeed in the Middle East if it abides by the rule of law, particularly international law and treaties to which it is signatory. There is one key opportunity to reverse a precipitous decline in moral authority: facilitating a just settlement of the Israel-Palestine conflict while abiding by international law and applicable UN resolutions.

The US needs to signal to the Middle East and the world a renewed American respect for international law by tackling the core regional conflict between Israel and Palestine. Key Israeli pundits have already stepped up a two-pronged disinformation campaign regarding Palestinian territories and their ongoing occupation. The first position is that returning an extremely limited control of Gaza to Palestinians represents major progress and even "land for peace." The second position is that portions of the West Bank, rebranded the new "Judea and Samaria" by former Israeli Ambassador to the UN Dore Gold and US-based Israeli lobbies, are non-negotiable in any future deal with Palestinians.

Is Gaza a "prize"? Informed analysis refutes the idea that an Israeli Gaza withdrawal is "progress." An isolated and densely populated Gaza with limited sovereignty is not a solution to the Palestinian refugees ousted during the creation of Israel in 1948. As Palestinian legislator Hanan Ashrawi clarified on Capitol Hill in February of 2004:

8. Rule of Law and Neocon Policy

"...it is very important that any removal of settlements from the Gaza Strip would not be seen as a license for Israel to consolidate its hold on the West Bank, to augment its settlements in the West Bank, to remove settlers from Gaza and add them to the West Bank settlements, or to claim that now that it has removed settlements, it can move the wall even further east and take more land and annex most of the West Bank. And the danger is precisely because the West Bank is the land of ideology for the settlers, not Gaza. They don't want Gaza. Remember, Rabin said he would like nothing better than to wake up one day and see that Gaza has sunk into the sea. Obviously, we should have told them, and at one time during negotiations, one of my colleagues said, "If we accept Gaza, what will you give us in return?" [3]

Key diplomatic maneuvers leading up to the Israeli occupation were unavailable until the release of previously classified information one year ago. Until January of 2004, it was common historical perception that the 1967 six-day war and subsequent Israeli seizure of the West Bank and Jerusalem were an "unavoidable response" to imminent Arab aggression. Yet previously classified data released in January 2004 by the Office of the Historian of the US State Department reveals desperate Egyptian diplomatic attempts to wind down the confrontation and repeated guarantees by Nasser to leaders in Washington that it would not strike first. The US estimated that these private Egyptian entreaties were intercepted and ultimately thwarted by Israel's preemptive air attacks on June 6 of 1967. [4] Palestinian refugees never judged Israel the justified new owner of the West Bank and entirety of Jerusalem. Official histories in the US no longer do either.

Return to the concept of "rule of law" in the Middle East will begin with America's firm commitment to returning lands expropriated by Israel in 1967 to Palestinians and aiding in negotiating the Right of Return and/or Israeli reparations to populations displaced in 1948.

American values will not lead toward continued financial support or partnership in the ethnic cleansing of Palestinians.

Settling the Israeli-Palestinian conflict in 2005 is a necessary moral precursor to any larger attempt to reform and develop the region. The US will continue to suffer a crisis of confidence, domestically and abroad, if US policies subvert international treaties, laws, and American values.

References

1."Working Group Report on Detainee Interrogations in the Global War on Terrorism: Assessment of Legal, Historical, Policy, and Operational Considerations," US Department of Defense, http://www.IRmep.org/military_0604.pdf

2.The James Baker Documents, The Nation http://www.thenation.com/doc.mhtml?i=20041101&s=bakerd ocs

3.The US Role in the Middle East Peace Process, Rayburn House Office Building, February 12, 2004 http://www.cnionline.org/hearings/ashrawi/transcript.htm

4.Foreign Relations, 1964-1968, Volume XIX, Arab-Israeli Crisis and War, 1967, Released by the Office of the Historian, Documents 129-148 US State Department in Foreign Relations, 1964-1968, Volume XIX, Arab-Israeli Crisis and War, 1967 http://www.state.gov/r/pa/ho/frus/johnsonlb/xix/28057.htm View a discussion of this information release at: rtsp://cspanrm.fplive.net/cspan/archive/iraq/iraq011204_stated ept.rm

9
Iran: The Imperative to Take Back American Policy

Institute for Research: Middle Eastern Policy analysis published September 17, 2004.

In 2002, Iran announced plans to build six nuclear power stations. As a signatory of the Nuclear Non-Proliferation Treaty (NPT), Iran can buy and operate centrifuges and other equipment needed for enriching uranium as long as it only uses the devices for nuclear power. NPT rules require that inspectors from the International Atomic Energy Agency (IAEA) be allowed into Iranian labs for verification purposes. Although the IAEA indicated on September 13, 2004 that officials were being allowed access to Iranian nuclear facilities, aspects of Iran's uranium enrichment efforts remain unclear.

Particles of weapons-grade enriched uranium were detected in Iran during IAEA inspections. Iran claimed contamination was present on imported equipment. According to Jane's Defence Weekly, IAEA inspectors reached a tentative conclusion that equipment smuggled through the network headed by Pakistani scientist AQ Khan arrived in Iran contaminated from previous enrichment. Other analysts believe the traces are damning evidence of a clandestine Iranian nuclear weapons program.

Whether or not Iran is currently pursuing nuclear weapons, American interests are best served if all nuclear proliferation in the Middle East is reversed. Unfortunately, recent US policies have only created conditions in which nuclear weapon acquisition is seen as a means of survival for countries on the neoconservative policy "target list."

From the Iranian perspective, Israel has not only successfully developed its own arsenal of nuclear weapons under a policy of "strategic ambiguity," it has also shaped US policy through the efforts of American neoconservatives with ties to the Israeli Likud party. American citizens must demand an effective counter-proliferation strategy toward Tehran that first eliminates the policy of "strategic ambiguity" operating in Tel Aviv and Washington.

In the Middle East, there is only one known nuclear power. Estimates of the Israeli arsenal vary widely, but Israel has successfully maintained a policy of "strategic ambiguity," neither admitting nor denying possession of nuclear weapons. This has allowed Israel to skirt NPT and US trade sanctions such as the Symington Amendment. (See Exhibit #1.)

Exhibit 1: USAF Estimates of Israeli Arsenal

Year	Estimates from Various Sources
1967	13 bombs
1969	5-6 bombs of 19 kilotons yield
1973	13 bombs, 20 nuclear missiles and development of a "suitcase bomb"
1974	3 nuclear-capable artillery battalions, each with 12 175mm tubes and total of 108 warheads; 10 bombs
1976	10-20 nuclear weapons
1980	200 bombs
1984	12-31 atomic bombs, 31 plutonium bombs, and 10 uranium bombs
1985	At least 100 nuclear bombs
1986	100-200 fission bombs and a number of fusion bombs
1991	50-60 to 200-300
1992	Greater than 200 bombs
1994	64-112 bombs @ 5 kg/warhead; 70-80 weapons, "a complete repertoire" (neutron bombs, nuclear mines, suitcase bombs, submarine-borne)
1996	60-80 plutonium weapons, maybe >100 assembles, ER variants, variable yields; possibly 200-300; 50-90 plutonium weapons, could have well over 135; 50-100 Jericho I and 30-50 Jericho II missiles.
1997	Greater than 400 deliverable thermonuclear and nuclear weapons

9. Iran: The Imperative to Take Back American Policy

Unfortunately, Israel's acquisition of an arsenal of tactical and strategic weapons and its ability to directly and indirectly create "facts on the ground" in the region now make it both the model and the primary motivation for other state actors.

According to Adam Shapiro, Israel's status makes future regional rebalancing inevitable:

"In the same way that Israel is promoting itself as a regional hegemon, as a regional superpower, it is getting to the point where other countries will seek to ally against Israel. And it should be noted that there is no alliance in the current formulation. Egypt, Jordan, if they are aligned with anyone, it is the United States. They are large recipients of American aid money and American military dollars. As such, they pose no threat whatsoever to Israel." (November 26, 2003, IRmep Capitol Hill forum)

However, Iran can legitimately assume that after Iraq, it is next in line on the Israeli (and therefore American) list of targets for military intervention. It need read no further than the US National Security Strategy and key neoconservative policy documents. (See Exhibit #2.)

Exhibit 2: Policies Developed and Implemented by Neoconservative Ideologues

Year	Policy	Defining Policy Document	Neoconservative Ideologues
1996	Invade Iraq, strike Syria, then Iran	**A Clean Break: A New Strategy for Securing the Realm** – Institute for Advanced Strategic and Political Studies	Richard Perle, Douglas Feith, David Wurmser
2000	Iran as a "threat to US interests in the Gulf," necessity for maintaining "forward bases in the region"	**Rebuilding America's Defenses** –Project for the New American Century	William Kristol, Robert Kagan, John Bolton
2002	Freeze "nuclear club" membership, "preemptive attacks" against transgressors	**The National Security Strategy** – National Security Council	Paul Wolfowitz

The past eight years of American actions have taught regional observers, including Iran, three significant lessons:

1. Opaque nuclear capability development and ambiguity can allow a small power to suddenly and securely enter the nuclear club;

2. Nascent nuclear states such as North Korea can deter attack from even the United States with only limited numbers of nuclear weapons;

3. A little understood extension of "Strategic Ambiguity" into the US allows Israeli lobbies and ideologues to successfully direct US military policy in the Middle East against threats to Israeli interests while plausibly denying it and claiming that Israeli's enemies are, in fact, America's own.

9. Iran: The Imperative to Take Back American Policy

From the Iranian government's perspective, right-wing Likud policies targeting Iran make it an urgent matter of survival to acquire an arsenal of tactical and strategic nuclear weapons as quickly as possible. From an American standpoint, the US cannot engage or even credibly threaten Tehran with international isolation unless America first tackles "strategic ambiguity" in Tel Aviv and Washington. Lifting the rhetorical smoke of "strategic ambiguity" reveals the vast differences between US and Israeli policy objectives in the region. (See Exhibit #3.)

Exhibit 3: State Regional Policy Objectives and Challenges

Country	Policy Objectives	Impediments/Challengers
Iran	Maintain sovereignty, territorial contiguity. Deter, repel, or respond to foreign aggressors.	US military presence on two fronts. Lack of tactical and strategic nuclear weapons.
Israel	Extend nuclear hegemony in the region. Maintain benefits of "strategic ambiguity." Defeat perceived rivals without appearing to do so.	Nuclear club entrants. International scrutiny, growing international pressure. Deteriorating "cover" for neoconservative policy implementation by the US.
United States	Secure global access to petroleum and natural gas reserves. Continuous petroleum and natural gas production. Elimination of WMD and forces driving proliferation in the region.	Widespread conflict driven by religious extremism. Terror attacks against energy production infrastructure. Inability to negotiate, form international coalitions, or be perceived as an "honest broker" in the region.

America's first step toward diffusing regional proliferation is dispersing the fog of "strategic ambiguity." If Israeli nuclear weapons and regional policies are the major catalyst of demand for weapons of mass destruction by other regional actors, Israel's operatives in the United States are clearly the fixative. Recent allegations about sensitive, classified documents on US policy toward Iran making their way from Undersecretary of Defense Douglas Feith's office to AIPAC, and then on to Israel, are only the most recent incident causing Americans to lose confidence and believe that Israeli-linked officials are compromising American interests. To date, Perle, Feith, and Wolfowitz, among other neoconservatives, have operated under an inky cloud of "strategic ambiguity" from which they claim efforts on behalf of Israel are in fact on behalf of America.

It is now time for America to "clean house" of the entire lot of compromised neoconservative advisors in order to assure both the American people and the international community that US actions in the region are a legitimate reflection of true American interests, rather than extensions of Israeli policy. America can no longer function or exert influence in the region unless it regains status as an "honest broker." Future policy in the region, including potential military actions, will suffer growing skepticism from American citizens now becoming aware of the curious and unpalatable linkages key administration advisors have to Israel.

Recommendations:

America's principal interest is to defuse all Middle East nuclear proliferation. Even the most limited use of tactical or nuclear weapons by any party in the petroleum-rich Middle East could throw the world into an unending economic depression. To avert nascent nuclear proliferation in the Middle East, the US must:

1. Demand a Public Nuclear Audit from Tel Aviv
Unless Congress drops decades of complicity in obscuring Israeli nuclear arms policy, it will never understand or constructively deal with the prime motivation for other regional states to acquire nuclear weapons. Congress must immediately recognize that Israel is a nuclear power and pressure it to join the NPT. An immediate IAEA audit of Israeli weapons and targeting data must commence.

2. Regional Disarmament Treaty

US interests are best served by a fully denuclearized Middle East. Neither perceived friends nor enemies should be allowed to maintain or further develop nuclear weapons. Toward this end, the US should apply pressure on Israel to dismantle its nuclear and other weapons of mass destruction under multinational observation. Other states can be legitimately pressured or forced to halt development programs if a verifiable regional treaty that also oversees the removal of Israel's arsenal is in effect.

3. Middle East Advisor Hiring Criteria

US advisors and policy makers lose credibility and effectiveness if they are perceived to function under Israeli influence. The administration should strive to purge "ambiguous" advisors and install competent appointees who can credibly represent US interests under the following criteria:

a) Appointees have not entered contractual, advisory, or other business relationships with governments of the region;

b) Appointees have no compromising regional ideological or religious affiliations which cloud or influence their decision-making;

c) Appointees are competent, regionally knowledgeable, and experienced in dealing with governments across the entire Middle East.

This may require that the administration pass over crowing legions of think-tank pundits, lobbyists, and candidates advanced by major campaign donors to once again reach for proven figures in business and academic circles.

By returning to the traditional American practice of hiring advisors and appointees who agree to serve at some sacrifice to other interests, America can again harness the energy of motivated and uncompromised patriots. Improving the quality of American advisors and appointees is critical for confronting the true proliferation dynamics of the region. Ending "strategic ambiguity" and returning to the pursuit of true American regional interests is the first step.

Appendix #1: A Clean Break

Following is a report prepared by The Institute for Advanced Strategic and Political Studies' "Study Group on a New Israeli Strategy Toward 2000." The main substantive ideas in this paper emerge from a discussion in which prominent opinion makers, including Richard Perle, James Colbert, Charles Fairbanks, Jr., Douglas Feith, Robert Loewenberg, David Wurmser, and Meyrav Wurmser, participated. The report, entitled "A Clean Break: A New Strategy for Securing the Realm," is the framework for a series of follow-up reports on strategy.

Israel has a large problem. Labor Zionism, which for 70 years has dominated the Zionist movement, has generated a stalled and shackled economy. Efforts to salvage Israel's socialist institutions—which include pursuing supranational over national sovereignty and pursuing a peace process that embraces the slogan, "New Middle East"—undermine the legitimacy of the nation and lead Israel into strategic paralysis and the previous government's "peace process." That peace process obscured the evidence of eroding national critical mass—including a palpable sense of national exhaustion—and forfeited strategic initiative. The loss of national critical mass was illustrated best by Israel's efforts to draw in the United States to sell unpopular policies domestically, to agree to negotiate sovereignty over its capital, and to respond with resignation to a spate of terror so intense and tragic that it deterred Israelis from engaging in normal daily functions, such as commuting to work in buses.

Benjamin Netanyahu's government comes in with a new set of ideas. While there are those who will counsel continuity, Israel has the opportunity to make a clean break; it can forge a peace process and strategy based on an entirely new intellectual foundation, one that restores strategic initiative and provides the nation the room to engage every possible energy on rebuilding Zionism, the starting point of which must be economic reform. To secure the nation's streets and borders in the immediate future, Israel can:

- Work closely with Turkey and Jordan to contain, destabilize, and roll back some of its most dangerous threats. This implies clean break from the slogan, "comprehensive peace" to a traditional concept of strategy based on balance of power.

- Change the nature of its relations with the Palestinians, including upholding the right of hot pursuit for self defense into all Palestinian areas and nurturing alternatives to Arafat's exclusive grip on Palestinian society.

- Forge a new basis for relations with the United States—stressing self-reliance, maturity, strategic cooperation on areas of mutual concern, and furthering values inherent to the West. This can only be done if Israel takes serious steps to terminate aid, which prevents economic reform.

This report is written with key passages of a possible speech marked TEXT, that highlight the clean break which the new government has an opportunity to make. The body of the report is the commentary explaining the purpose and laying out the strategic context of the passages.

A New Approach to Peace

Early adoption of a bold, new perspective on peace and security is imperative for the new prime minister. While the previous government, and many abroad, may emphasize "land for peace"—which placed Israel in the position of cultural, economic, political, diplomatic, and military retreat—the new government can promote Western values and traditions. Such an approach, which will be well received in the United States, includes "peace for peace," "peace through strength" and self reliance: the balance of power.

A new strategy to seize the initiative can be introduced:

TEXT:

We have for four years pursued peace based on a New Middle East. We in Israel cannot play innocents abroad in a world that is not innocent. Peace depends on the character and behavior of our foes. We live in a dangerous neighborhood, with fragile states and bitter rivalries. Displaying moral ambivalence between the effort to build a Jewish state and the desire to annihilate it by trading "land for peace" will not secure "peace now." Our claim to the land —to which we have clung for hope for 2000 years--is legitimate and noble. It is not within our own power, no matter how much we concede, to make peace unilaterally. Only the unconditional acceptance by Arabs of our rights, especially in their territorial dimension, "peace for peace," is a solid basis for the future.

Israel's quest for peace emerges from, and does not replace, the pursuit of its ideals. The Jewish people's hunger for human rights—burned into their identity by a 2000-year-old dream to live free in their own land—informs the concept of peace and reflects continuity of values with Western and Jewish tradition. Israel can now embrace negotiations, but as means, not ends, to pursue those ideals and demonstrate national steadfastness. It can challenge police states; enforce compliance of agreements; and insist on minimal standards of accountability.

<u>Securing the Northern Border</u>

Syria challenges Israel on Lebanese soil. An effective approach, and one with which American can sympathize, would be if Israel seized the strategic initiative along its northern borders by engaging Hezbollah, Syria, and Iran, as the principal agents of aggression in Lebanon, including by:

- striking Syria's drug-money and counterfeiting infrastructure in Lebanon, all of which focuses on Razi Qanan.

- paralleling Syria's behavior by establishing the precedent that Syrian territory is not immune to attacks emanating from Lebanon by Israeli proxy forces.

- striking Syrian military targets in Lebanon, and should that prove insufficient, striking at select targets in Syria proper.

Israel also can take this opportunity to remind the world of the nature of the Syrian regime. Syria repeatedly breaks its word. It violated numerous agreements with the Turks, and has betrayed the United States by continuing to occupy Lebanon in violation of the Taef agreement in 1989. Instead, Syria staged a sham election, installed a quisling regime, and forced Lebanon to sign a "Brotherhood Agreement" in 1991, that terminated Lebanese sovereignty. And Syria has begun colonizing Lebanon with hundreds of thousands of Syrians, while killing tens of thousands of its own citizens at a time, as it did in only three days in 1983 in Hama.

Under Syrian tutelage, the Lebanese drug trade, for which local Syrian military officers receive protection payments, flourishes. Syria's regime supports the terrorist groups operationally and financially in Lebanon and on its soil. Indeed, the Syrian-controlled Bekaa Valley in Lebanon has become for terror what the Silicon Valley has become for computers. The Bekaa Valley has become one of the main distribution sources, if not production points, of the "supernote"—counterfeit US currency so well done that it is impossible to detect.

Text:

Negotiations with repressive regimes like Syria's require cautious realism. One cannot sensibly assume the other side's good faith. It is dangerous for Israel to deal naively with a regime murderous of its own people, openly aggressive toward its neighbors, criminally involved with international drug traffickers and counterfeiters, and supportive of the most deadly terrorist organizations.

Given the nature of the regime in Damascus, it is both natural and moral that Israel abandon the slogan "comprehensive peace" and move to contain Syria, drawing attention to its weapons of mass destruction program, and rejecting "land for peace" deals on the Golan Heights.

Moving to a Traditional Balance of Power Strategy

TEXT:

We must distinguish soberly and clearly friend from foe. We must make sure that our friends across the Middle East never doubt the solidity or value of our friendship.

Israel can shape its strategic environment, in cooperation with Turkey and Jordan, by weakening, containing, and even rolling back Syria. This effort can focus on removing Saddam Hussein from power in Iraq—an important Israeli strategic objective in its own right—as a means of foiling Syria's regional ambitions. Jordan has challenged Syria's regional ambitions recently by suggesting the restoration of the Hashemites in Iraq. This has triggered a Jordanian-Syrian rivalry to which Asad has responded by stepping up efforts to destabilize the Hashemite Kingdom, including using infiltrations. Syria recently signaled that it and Iran might prefer a weak, but barely surviving Saddam, if only to undermine and humiliate Jordan in its efforts to remove Saddam.

But Syria enters this conflict with potential weaknesses: Damascus is too preoccupied with dealing with the threatened new regional equation to permit distractions of the Lebanese flank. And Damascus fears that the "natural axis" with Israel on one side, central Iraq and Turkey on the other, and Jordan in the center would squeeze and detach Syria from the Saudi Peninsula. For Syria, this could be the prelude to a redrawing of the map of the Middle East which would threaten Syria's territorial integrity.

Since Iraq's future could affect the strategic balance in the Middle East profoundly, it would be understandable that Israel has an interest in supporting the Hashemites in their efforts to redefine Iraq, including such measures as: visiting Jordan as the first official state visit, even before a visit to the United States, of the new Netanyahu government; supporting King Hussein by providing him with some tangible security measures to protect his regime against Syrian subversion; encouraging—through influence in the US business community—investment in Jordan to structurally shift Jordan's economy away from dependence on Iraq; and diverting Syria's attention by using Lebanese opposition elements to destabilize Syrian control of Lebanon.

Most important, it is understandable that Israel has an interest supporting diplomatically, militarily and operationally Turkey's and Jordan's actions against Syria, such as securing tribal alliances with Arab tribes that cross into Syrian territory and are hostile to the Syrian ruling elite.

King Hussein may have ideas for Israel in bringing its Lebanon problem under control. The predominantly Shia population of southern Lebanon has been tied for centuries to the Shia leadership in Najf, Iraq rather than Iran. Were the Hashemites to control Iraq, they could use their influence over Najf to help Israel wean the south Lebanese Shia away from Hezbollah, Iran, and Syria. Shia retain strong ties to the Hashemites: the Shia venerate foremost the Prophet's family, the direct descendant of which—and in whose veins the blood of the Prophet flows—is King Hussein.

Changing the Nature of Relations with the Palestinians

Israel has a chance to forge a new relationship between itself and the Palestinians. First and foremost, Israel's efforts to secure its streets may require hot pursuit into Palestinian-controlled areas, a justifiable practice with which Americans can sympathize.

A key element of peace is compliance with agreements already signed. Therefore, Israel has the right to insist on compliance, including closing Orient House and disbanding Jibril Rujoub's operatives in Jerusalem. Moreover, Israel and the United States can establish a Joint Compliance Monitoring Committee to study periodically whether the PLO meets minimum standards of compliance, authority and responsibility, human rights, and judicial and fiduciary accountability.

TEXT:

We believe that the Palestinian Authority must be held to the same minimal standards of accountability as other recipients of US foreign aid. A firm peace cannot tolerate repression and injustice. A regime that cannot fulfill the most rudimentary obligations to its own people cannot be counted upon to fulfill its obligations to its neighbors.

Israel has no obligations under the Oslo agreements if the PLO does not fulfill its obligations. If the PLO cannot comply with these minimal standards, then it can be neither a hope for the future nor a proper interlocutor for present. To prepare for this, Israel may want to cultivate alternatives to Arafat's base of power. Jordan has ideas on this.

To emphasize the point that Israel regards the actions of the PLO problematic, but not the Arab people, Israel might want to consider making a special effort to reward friends and advance human rights among Arabs. Many Arabs are willing to work with Israel; identifying and helping them are important. Israel may also find that many of her neighbors, such as Jordan, have problems with Arafat and may want to cooperate. Israel may also want to better integrate its own Arabs.

Forging A New US-Israeli Relationship

In recent years, Israel invited active US intervention in Israel's domestic and foreign policy for two reasons: to overcome domestic opposition to "land for peace" concessions the Israeli public could not digest, and to lure Arabs—through money, forgiveness of past sins, and access to US weapons—to negotiate. This strategy, which required funneling American money to repressive and aggressive regimes, was risky, expensive, and very costly for both the US and Israel, and placed the United States in roles is should neither have nor want.

Israel can make a clean break from the past and establish a new vision for the US-Israeli partnership based on self-reliance, maturity and mutuality—not one focused narrowly on territorial disputes. Israel's new strategy—based on a shared philosophy of peace through strength—reflects continuity with Western values by stressing that Israel is self-reliant, does not need US troops in any capacity to defend it, including on the Golan Heights, and can manage its own affairs. Such self-reliance will grant Israel greater freedom of action and remove a significant lever of pressure used against it in the past.

To reinforce this point, the Prime Minister can use his forthcoming visit to announce that Israel is now mature enough to cut itself free immediately from at least US economic aid and loan guarantees at least, which prevent economic reform. [Military aid is separated for the moment until adequate arrangements can be made to ensure that Israel will not encounter supply problems in the means to defend itself]. As outlined in another Institute report, Israel can become self-reliant only by, in a bold stroke rather than in increments, liberalizing its economy, cutting taxes, relegislating a free-processing zone, and selling-off public lands and enterprises—moves which will electrify and find support from a broad bipartisan spectrum of key pro-Israeli Congressional leaders, including Speaker of the House Newt Gingrich.

Israel can under these conditions better cooperate with the US to counter real threats to the region and the West's security. Mr. Netanyahu can highlight his desire to cooperate more closely with the United States on anti-missile defense in order to remove the threat of blackmail which even a weak and distant army can pose to either state. Not only would such cooperation on missile defense counter a tangible physical threat to Israel's survival, but it would broaden Israel's base of support among many in the United States Congress who may know little about Israel, but care very much about missile defense. Such broad support could be helpful in the effort to move the US embassy in Israel to Jerusalem.

To anticipate US reactions and plan ways to manage and constrain those reactions, Prime Minister Netanyahu can formulate the policies and stress themes he favors in language familiar to the Americans by tapping into themes of American administrations during the Cold War which apply well to Israel. If Israel wants to test certain propositions that require a benign American reaction, then the best time to do so is before November, 1996.

Conclusions: Transcending the Arab-Israeli Conflict

TEXT: Israel will not only contain its foes; it will transcend them.

Notable Arab intellectuals have written extensively on their perception of Israel's floundering and loss of national identity. This perception has invited attack, blocked Israel from achieving true peace, and offered hope for those who would destroy Israel. The previous strategy, therefore, was leading the Middle East toward another Arab-Israeli war. Israel's new agenda can signal a clean break by abandoning a policy which assumed exhaustion and allowed strategic retreat by reestablishing the principle of preemption, rather than retaliation alone and by ceasing to absorb blows to the nation without response.

Israel's new strategic agenda can shape the regional environment in ways that grant Israel the room to refocus its energies back to where they are most needed: to rejuvenate its national idea, which can only come through replacing Israel's socialist foundations with a more sound footing; and to overcome its "exhaustion," which threatens the survival of the nation.

Ultimately, Israel can do more than simply manage the Arab-Israeli conflict though war. No amount of weapons or victories will grant Israel the peace its seeks. When Israel is on a sound economic footing, and is free, powerful, and healthy internally, it will no longer simply manage the Arab-Israeli conflict; it will transcend it. As a senior Iraqi opposition leader said recently: "Israel must rejuvenate and revitalize its moral and intellectual leadership. It is an important—if not the most important—element in the history of the Middle East." Israel—proud, wealthy, solid, and strong—would be the basis of a truly new and peaceful Middle East.

Participants in the Study Group on "A New Israeli Strategy Toward 2000"

Richard Perle, American Enterprise Institute, Study Group Leader

James Colbert, Jewish Institute for National Security Affairs

Charles Fairbanks, Jr., Johns Hopkins University/SAIS

Douglas Feith, Feith and Zell Associates

Robert Loewenberg, President, Institute for Advanced Strategic and Political Studies

Jonathan Torop, The Washington Institute for Near East Policy

David Wurmser, Institute for Advanced Strategic and Political Studies, Meyrav Wurmser, Johns Hopkins University

Appendix #2: About the IRmep

The Institute for Research Middle Eastern Policy (IRmep) is an independent nonprofit public policy research "think tank" headquartered in Washington, D.C. Founded in 2002, the institute provides balanced, relevant, and actionable research and recommendations for US policy in the Middle East. IRmep educates US policymakers, Non-Governmental Organizations (NGOs), and the mass media. The IRmep analyst team research agenda focuses on areas of critical concern:

1. Peaceful settlement of regional and international disputes by returning the US to its higher role, that of a just and engaged regional influence;

2. The role of US merchandise and service exports in the development and transformation of regional infrastructure;

3. Facilitating and increasing bilateral foreign direct and passive investment;

4. Inter-regional education, knowledge, culture, and intellectual capital transfers;

5. Security and defense strategy that confronts the true underlying causes of terrorism and the real roots of conflict.

IRmep produces research, publications, media commentary, focused educational events, and research tour programs to the Middle East. The heart of our work is academically, not ideologically, driven research. The IRmep network of analysts is composed of experienced research academics with reviewers in the business and diplomatic communities. IRmep analysts are bound by a single common tie: the unbiased study and analysis of sovereign American interests in the region.

IRmep's mission is to produce accurate, relevant, actionable research and recommendations to key policy makers identifying US interests in the Middle East and the means for achieving them.

By leveraging a network of credible academics with domain expertise, IRmep policy research avoids damaging ideological bias and unproductive frameworks when analyzing the region.

IRmep's funding comes from a broad range of corporate, foundation, and individual donors that wish to see US policy in the region become more responsive to the interests of all Americans.

Our effectiveness derives from the IRmep research agenda and content distribution strategy. IRmep focuses the policymaker spotlight back toward issues of importance to Americans. IRmep research projects already chartered or published include:

1. US Merchandise Exports to the Arab Market
40,000 copies published and distributed in the brief titled "Dividends of Fear, America's $94 Billion Dollar Arab Market Export Loss." Examination of best-case and worst-case US merchandise export forecasts over 1998-2007 period. Recommendations for corporations and policymakers to reverse US export share declines.

2. UN Approaches to Iraq and Palestine
UN briefing paper on the strategic opportunity to "bundle" UN peacekeeping missions in Iraq and Palestine toward a regionally relevant security solution.

3. Service Exports to the Arab Market
Model and forecast of US service exports. Recommendations for increasing US participation in key segments for infrastructure building and transition projects.

4. American National Security Strategy in the Middle East
Review of regional US military strategies, intelligence, and interests.

5. American Interests in the Middle East: A Policy Overhaul
US Middle East Policy Formulation Overhaul Project brief on
US regional interests, bridge analysis, and recommendations.

6. US/Arab Academic Exchange Update
Analysis of declining number of Arab foreign students in the
US higher education system. Impact on future diplomatic,
commercial, and cultural relations.

Each IRmep policy research project has a custom content
distribution strategy engineered to obtain the maximum
response from policy makers and key stakeholders. IRmep
content has been presented to the 108th Congress and Senate,
White House, Department of State, Department of Commerce,
UN Security Council and General Assembly, and Department
of Homeland Security.

IRmep content about commercial interests has been distributed
to over 3,000 select corporations, industry associations and
lobbies, chambers of commerce, and trade magazines, as well
as investment banks and development-oriented NGOs. IRmep
content and analysis for the public has quickly gained ground
in the mainstream media and Internet. IRmep has appeared on
CBS MarketWatch, Associated Press, Gannett News,
Financial Times of London, Arab News, The Boston Globe,
The Guardian, San Jose Mercury News, The Daily Star of
Lebanon, and broadcast media such as the Radio America
Network. IRmep.org is now the #1 site for content on
"Middle Eastern Policy" in the world's top relevancy-based
search engine, Google.com.

Institute for Research Middle Eastern Policy Inc. is an IRS recognized tax exempt 501 (c) (3) non-profit. To become a supporter, review the current research agenda, or arrange for consultations and speaking engagements, please contact the Institute for Research Middle Eastern Policy headquarters in Washington, D.C. at (202) 342-7325 or visit us on the web at http://www.IRmep.org.

Institute for Research: Middle Eastern Policy

Quick Order Form
Fax orders: 202-318-8009
Email:info@IRmep.org
Web: www.IRmep.org
Mail: IRmep
PO Box 32041
Washington, DC, 20007

Please send the following number of units of the book **Neocon Middle East Policy: The "Clean Break" Plan Damage Assessment**. I understand I may return any of them for a full refund within two weeks of purchase for any reason, no questions asked.

Books (units)	
Price	$9.95
Book units x Price	$
Shipping & Handling*	$
Total	$

*Shipping by air: US: $4 for the first book and $2.00 for each additional book.

Shipping/Billing Information
Name:_____
Shipping address:_____
City:_____State____Zip_____
Telephone:_____
Email address:_____

Payment Information
☐Check (enclosed) ☐Visa ☐MasterCard ☐American Express
Card number:_____
Name on card:_____ Expiration date:__/__/__
Security code:_____(3 or 4 digit number above signature)
Card billing address if different than
above:_____
_____